The New Factory Thinker

BILL BISHOP

ISBN-13: 978-1499641073

ISBN-10: 1499641079

CONTENTS

Preface: New Thinking For A New Marketplace   1

Introduction: The Singularity Is Here   11

SECTION 1: THE NEW FACTORY MARKETPLACE

1   The New Marketplace Realities   19

2   Harry: An Old Factory Thinker   33

3   Harry: A New Factory Thinker   37

4   The Old Factory Model   43

5   The New Factory Model   51

SECTION 2: BUILDING YOUR NEW FACTORY

6   Step 1: One Customer Type   63

7   Step 2.1: The Big Goal   67

8   Step 2.2: The Big Problem   73

9   Step 2.3: The Signature Solution   79

10   Step 3: Free Value   87

11   Step 4: Membership Program   93

12   Step 5: One-Stop Store   103

SECTION 3: NEW FACTORY VALUE CREATION

13   Less Resources   113

14   Under-Utilized Resources   119

15   Togetherness   123

16   Integration   129

17   Objectivity   135

18   Transformation   141

19   Emotional Value   147

20   Empowerment   153

21   Conceptual Value   159

22   Interfaces   165

23   Teaching   171

24   Curating   177

25   Entertaining   181

SECTION 4: NEW FACTORY FOUNDATIONS

26   Value Hubs   187

27   Ideas   195

28   Weightless   199

29   Slow   205

30   Transcendence   209

31   Well-Being   213

32   The New Factory Future   215

SECTION 5: APPENDICES

Acknowledgements   219

Bibliography   223

About Bill Bishop   229

PREFACE

NEW THINKING FOR A NEW MARKETPLACE

When I wrote another $700 check for the lease on our mailing machine, I realized the future had caught up with me and I hadn't seen it coming.

Three years earlier, I thought I was a genius. I had contracts to publish newsletters and magazines for more than 100 clients. My most lucrative revenue source was mailing out the publications to our clients' customers and prospects. To do this, we had leased a high-speed mailing machine that cranked out hundreds of letters per hour. It was a pricey piece of equipment, but I loved it. Every letter that went through the machine meant one thing: money. The more letters, the more money. The sound of the mailing machine in high gear was music to my ears.

But then market conditions changed. Business owners migrated away from printed marketing tools to their digital counter-parts. Like a slow death, the demand for my printed products declined day by day. The lovely sound of the mailing machine churning out letters became less frequent and I by extension less happy. Then one day, the finance company called to see if I wanted to re-lease the machine for another six years. After some pondering, I agreed because I still had a fair bit of mailing business even if it was on the decline. I figured there was nothing else to do.

Three years later, the mailing machine sat silent in the mailing room. No one sent out printed newsletters anymore. Everything had gone digital. But there I was handing over $700 month after month.

This nasty experience taught me a lesson. When you run a business, the future probably won't be the same as the past. When you make a long-term commitment to an asset like a mailing machine, there's no guarantee that resource will be required in the future. But you'll still be on the hook for it and that can cost you a lot of money.

I realize now that the mailing machine was a manifestation of my old factory thinking at the time. My business mind was running on an old operating system that had been programmed into the collective consciousness of our culture at the start of the Industrial Revolution. With a brain wired for old factory thinking, I didn't see how the world was changing and, as a result, I made bad business decisions. In this case my erroneous thinking cost me thousands of dollars.

That's why I wrote this book. To help you recognize your own old factory thinking and re-wire your mind so you can survive and succeed in the new factory marketplace. To illustrate what I mean, consider these three scenarios:

Scenario 1. You're in a meeting at Apple in 1998. The top executives are brainstorming ideas to sell more computers. Suggestions are bandied about: "Maybe we should lower the price of the Mac? Maybe we should increase our advertising budget? Maybe we should expand our retail network?" Then someone at the back of the room, a newly-appointed executive, puts up her hand and says: "I think we should sell music." The question is: Would you have voted for or against that idea?

Scenario 2. In 1990, you meet Howard Schultz. He's full of enthusiasm about his idea for a company called Starbucks. He tells you his vision: "We're going to get people to pay $5 for a cup of coffee." The question is: In 1990, when the average cup of coffee was 50 cents, would you have supported Schultz's idea for a $5 cup of coffee?

Scenario 3. In the 1990s, you attend a meeting in Palo Alto. Two guys have invented something called a "search engine" and it's attracting lots of users. The inventors want to give their company a name. Someone suggests they call the company "Google." The question is: Would you have voted for or against that name?

Personally I would have voted no to all three ideas. In hindsight, it's tempting to say I would have voted yes, but I know I would have voted them down. My experience as a business coach tells me that most people would have voted no as well. Not because they lack intelligence or imagination, but because their mind is wired for the marketplace of the past, not the marketplace of the future. This is a huge problem because this old kind of thinking, what I call old factory thinking, stops them from achieving their full potential. It can also lead to unnecessary economic hardship for millions of people.

How we currently think about business has become obsolete. For the past 200 years, the Industrial Revolution wired our minds to think in a certain way, specifically like an assembly line: linear, hierarchical and efficiency-focused. It led us to believe that increasing consumption is the primary objective of the economy and that the key to success in the marketplace is to produce and sell as many products and services as possible. Our industrial, assembly-line minds also view the marketplace as a competitive battlefield where resources are scarce. This kind of thinking has worked so well for so long it has become the unquestioned mental template for success.

But old factory thinking is now obsolete because the economy and the marketplace have changed on a fundamental level. It has changed from an *assembly-line* economy to a *value hub* economy. The industrial assembly line has been replaced by the Internet, a global network of connected relationships, as the economy's dominant means of production.

This shift from an assembly line economy (old factory) to a value hub economy (new factory) is causing unprecedented and irreversible changes. Increased global competition is driving down margins on traditional products and services. This is forcing old factory companies to cut costs, often by replacing human employees with computers and robots. Many old factory companies have been forced out of business or marginalized. In addition, the psychology of consumers has changed. Empowered by new technology and exposed to an ever-increasing volume of information, they see the world through new eyes and behave differently in the marketplace. Ironically, the same technology that marketers use to reach consumers has also made it easier for them to hide from marketers, driving up the cost of sales. Under these conditions, old factory thinking doesn't work anymore. That's why I wrote this book: to teach you a new way of thinking that's more appropriate for the world we live in today.

Many of the issues and ideas discussed in this book will make you uncomfortable. Having your established way of thinking challenged is not fun. You might be scared about what's coming and hope it won't happen. You might worry about your business, your job, or your family's future. But you'll learn that new factory thinking is much more exciting and invigorating than old factory thinking. You'll realize you've placed unnecessary limitations on yourself. You'll understand that old factory thinking has been holding you back from achieving your full potential. You'll discover that greater success will come, not from working harder (you already work hard enough!) or even from working smarter. You'll discover that greater success will only happen when you transform your way of thinking on a fundamental level.

Using new factory thinking, you'll experience an explosion of ideas about how to provide new, more profitable kinds of value in the marketplace. You'll redefine what "value" means, and come to appreciate that in the new factory marketplace, value and wealth are being created in ways that were unimaginable in the old factory economy. You'll also see that building your new factory is also easy and fun.

The first step towards new factory thinking is to admit you currently engage in old factory thinking. Being brutally honest, you accept that your mind is programmed for the past, not the future. To see what I mean, let's review the three scenarios presented at the start of the chapter.

First, the story about Apple. When someone suggested they sell music, the natural reaction was negative. Why would we, a computer company, get into the music business? That's a different industry. That's not our area of expertise. We're a *computer* company, not a *music* company. Caught up in a limited self-definition (we're a computer company), most Apple people rejected the idea at first. But of course, we know now it was a brilliant idea. By branching out into music, Apple became a totally different kind of company. Once they broke through the "computer-only" barrier, they no longer placed restrictions on what they could or could not provide to their customers. This positive experience opened their minds to many other value creation possibilities such as iPhones, tablets, apps, movies, and e-books. Of course, there never were any real restrictions. The restrictions were only in their mind. There was no law stopping them from expanding into other industries: Just old factory thinking.

So when someone suggests you could provide value that falls outside your industry or product/service category, stop before you trash the idea. Notice your old factory thinking. You see, in the value hub economy, it doesn't matter what industry you're in. Your customers don't care. Only you care. In fact, in the value hub economy, traditional industry definitions are irrelevant. Ask yourself, what industry is Apple in? Can you say they're in the computer industry or the music industry? Are they in the telecommunications industry? In the value hub economy, it doesn't matter. Apple is its own industry. They're in the industry of creating value for their customers, no matter what that means.

Now to the Starbuck's story. In 1990, most people rejected Schultz's vision of a $5 cup of coffee. "Why would anyone pay $5 for a cup of coffee when you can get it for 50 cents?" they asked. Old factory thinkers couldn't imagine such a scenario so they didn't try to figure it out. But Schultz believed that "if we build it they will come." And indeed they do. Today, millions of people line up every day to pay $5 for a cup of coffee.

This kind of old factory thinking is common. When I suggest to business owners that their customers might pay 10 times more for something, they scoff. "Our customers will never pay more, certainly not 10 times more," they say. Then I ask them: "Pay 10 times more for what?" They can't see the opportunity because they're stuck in old factory thinking. Their old factory industry is so competitive and commoditized that, in their mind, price is the only point of differentiation. Their customers demand the lowest price and they try to provide it. So when I suggest their customers might pay ten times more, they can't imagine it. Their brains are just not wired to see the possibility.

Let's turn to the third story about Google. You can kid yourself, but I bet you would have voted against calling the company Google. You would have said: "That's a crazy name. It doesn't mean anything. It's weird. No one will get it. It will make us look foolish. It's too risky."

I used to be like that. When I started writing books, I gave them boring titles. I was trying to establish my credentials as an expert by being serious and conservative. But this old factory thinking stopped my books from standing out in the marketplace. Then I wrote a book with the title *How To Sell A Lobster*. The funny name worked. I've sold more than a million copies.

The lesson is: The 200-year-old-factory era wired our minds for conformity and conventionality. Being bland and boring worked best in a hierarchical society. Blending in and keeping a low profile was safer. Doing something strange or bizarre meant public scorn or even jail. Think of Oscar Wilde or Lenny Bruce. But in the new factory marketplace, being plain and boring means marginalization and failure. In today's entertainment-rich marketplace your customers are being amused 24/7 in a myriad of ways using a multitude of media. If you don't do something dramatic to catch their attention, you'll never emerge from the pack. So when someone suggests you put a picture of a giraffe on your website or call your company a name like ShoeLace or Flunky-Fest, think twice before you run the idea into the ground. Pause, notice your old factory thinking, and consider the potential upside of the strange, the odd, and the peculiar.

I love these three new factory scenarios because they cut through self-deception. Most of us believe we're forward-thinking and open minded, but it's simply not the case. When given an idea to create value outside our normal parameters, we often reject the idea. When it's suggested our customers might pay 10 times more, we disparage the notion. And when given the option to do something wild and crazy, we cringe at the possibility. That's just the way our minds are wired. From birth we have been conditioned for old factory thinking.

The lessons learned from Apple, Starbucks and Google is that new factory thinking works better these days. That's why we need to change how we think in a myriad of ways:

- Instead of thinking about how to get our customers to consume *more* resources, we need to think about how our customers can get better results using *less* resources.
- Instead of thinking in a linear and fragmented fashion, we need to think spatially and holistically.
- Instead of focusing exclusively on tangible products and services, we need to focus more of our attention on providing intangible value.
- Instead of being salespeople making a sales pitch, we need to

provide value during the sales process.

• Instead of creating a product or service once, we need to be continuous value creators.

• We need to focus more on what we know and less on what we do, and then turn our knowledge and wisdom into new forms of value.

• Most importantly, we need to be comfortable with continuous change, and re-configure our businesses and our thinking in order to welcome change as an opportunity not a threat.

Taken together, these elements of new factory thinking represent a radical re-arrangement of how we see the world and our role in it. Sadly, many people will not want to change their way of thinking and will fail in the new factory marketplace. Others will see the writing on the wall and make the effort to change. I'm hoping you're one of those people. If you are, let's get started.

INTRODUCTION

THE SINGULARITY IS HERE

In the late 1970s, a good friend got me a job in the computer department at a drug wholesaling company. I was responsible for operating a room-size mainframe computer linked to 300-plus drug stores across the country where pharmacists filled out prescriptions using a computer terminal. Though basic by today's standards, the system was a massive leap in productivity and capability. The pharmacists loved the system because it did in seconds what used to take them hours to accomplish.

During the 18 months I worked there, I got an inside look into the consequences, both good and bad, that advances in technology can have in the marketplace. Coincidentally at the same time, I was reading *The Medium Is The Message,* a book by Marshall McLuhan. I was digesting his thesis that new technology has an unpredictable and irreversible effect on how humans think, work and interact with each other.

I observed that the pharmacists were completely dependent on our computer system. One morning the system crashed and within seconds all the phones lines started ringing. The pharmacist couldn't fill their prescriptions and business had ground to a halt. Fortunately I rebooted the system in 45 minutes, but the lesson was clear. The pharmacists were completely dependent on this new technology. This dependency was underscored a month later when a fire broke out in our building. The smoke fried our computers and shut down the system for three days. The pharmacists were apoplectic but there was nothing they could do. They couldn't revert back to the previous manual system. That was the irreversible part Marshall McLuhan talked about.

Another consequence of this new technology became evident. The system was created by the drug wholesaler to monopolize the marketplace. They gave the computer terminals to the pharmacists for free, and once they started using it, they bought 98% of their drugs from our company. The pharmacists could still buy from other wholesalers, but it was a lot harder and more time-consuming, so they didn't bother. The other companies were locked out of the market. As you'll read in this book, I've coined a phrase for this type of monopoly: I call it an "alpha network."

I also had a first-hand lesson in Moore's law that states that computers double in speed every 18 months while becoming smaller and less expensive. The GEAC 8000 computer we used was twice as fast and less expensive than the GEAC 500/800 computer used the previous year. The GEAC 8000 computer was also smaller and had more capabilities. Since that time, I've kept track of this progression. Today my smart phone has 100,000 times more processing speed than the GEAC mainframe that filled a large room back in 1979.

This experience taught me that it's folly to ignore the impact of technology on our lives. If you run a business, it's likely something will happen in the near future that will have a disruptive impact on your business model. A new technology might undermine your business. A new competitor might change the power balance in your industry. Consumers might grow bored of what you're selling and flock to something new. Political and economic conditions might change and throw into question the viability of your industry. It's impossible to predict what specific changes will happen but you can be certain that change will come.

Change will happen because the singularity is here. I use this expression with thanks to Ray Kurzweil who wrote a book called *The Singularity Is Near.* Kurzweil is an inventor and a futurist who's worth listening to. Some people refuse to listen to his message but they close their ears at their peril. Kurzweil's message is simple: The exponential growth of computer processing speed and power will continue (Moore's Law), but the pace of this growth will be much greater in the coming decade.

To visualize this trend, think about the doubling of integers, starting with 1. The sequence goes 1, 2, 4, 8, 16, 32, 64, 128, 256, 512, 1014…. At first the increase per generation is relatively modest. For example, the increase in real terms from 4 to 8 is only four. Even the increase from 64 to 128 is only 64. But when you get further along in the sequence, the increase per generation becomes astronomical. For instance, within 22 generations, the sequence becomes: 1,048,576 to 2,097,152 to 4,194,304 to 8,388,608. At this point, the increase per generation is in the millions.

This is what is happening to computers today. Back in the '80s and '90s, computers sped up relatively slowly every 18 months: 1, 2, 4, 8, 16, 32, 64, 128, 256, 512, 1014…. Now they speed up by millions every 18 months: 1,048,576 to 2,097,152 to 4,194,304 to 8,388,608. In a few years, computers will speed up by billions every 18 months: 17,179,869,184 to 34,359,738,368 to 68,719,476,736. And then they will speed up by trillions every 18 months.

In their book *The Second Machine Age*, Erik Brynjolfsson and

Andrew McAfee use a good analogy to illustrate this concept in non-mathematical terms. Get out a chessboard. On the first square, place one piece of rice. Then put twice that amount of rice on the next square, and then twice that much on the third square. Keep doing this until you have completed the 64 squares. Now ask yourself: How big is the pile of rice on the 64th square?

Before I give you the answer, consider this. As you pile up the rice square by square, the first half of the chessboard is quite manageable. Even on the 32nd square, you still have a relatively small pile of rice. But when you get to the second half of the board, the piles get really big, and then even bigger. By the time you get to the 64th square, your pile of rice will be the size of Mount Everest (no kidding).

That's what's happening with computers. They've doubled in speed and capability for the past four decades, but it's been manageable because we were still on the first half of the chessboard. Now we've entered the second half of the board and the annual progression is accelerating beyond all previous experience. Each year, the progress of computers, and their effect on our economy and society, will exceed all of the progress achieved in all the previous years. That's why I say, "You ain't seen nothing yet," when it comes to technology-related change.

So what's this got to do with you and your business? Everything. It's not just that your computer will run faster, and that you will have more apps to play with on your smart phone; the impact will run much deeper. As Marshall McLuhan said: The medium is the message. It's not what we do with technology, or what we communicate with technology that matters; it's how the technology changes our society and us as human beings.

As computer-processing speed increases faster and faster, you, me, your family, your community, your company, your industry, and the whole world will be taken for a ride. It will be like a roller coaster that keeps picking up speed. Everything will change more rapidly and most of that change will be unpredictable. That's what Kurzweil means by the singularity. We're about to reach a point beyond which change will happen so fast and so unpredictably that we won't be able to plan for the future.

That's why it's important to design a business or career that is future-proof. If you use old factory thinking—which is based on planning your future around specific products and services—you take a huge risk. That model worked in the past when the future was more predictable and slower to change. You could spread out the risk of your capital investment over years, if not decades. Now however, if you use that model the odds will be against you.

But if you build a new factory—structured as a value hub—the odds will be in your favor. You'll be able to change and adapt your business on a day-by-day, even minute-by-minute basis, without needing to pull up roots. Like a sturdy oak tree, your new factory will grow tall and strong no matter how much the wind blows or from what direction.

Reading Kurzweil's book was both exhilarating and terrifying. As an entrepreneur, I revel in disruptive innovation. When I see disruption I see opportunity. But what if there is too much disruption? What if the world changes too fast? Kurzweil projects that within 20 years, a computer the size of your smart phone will have more processing power than the brains of everyone who ever lived times a trillion!

And that's not even the scary part. He also conjectures that at a certain point, computers will start designing and building their own progeny, and at that point, we lowly humans will not understand or be able to keep up with the technological advances they're creating. It's at that point the ultimate singularity will have arrived.

So that's frightening. And maybe it won't happen exactly like that. But it's certain, over the next decade; computers will become faster and smarter. More of us will become connected to each other, and just like the pharmacists, we'll use technology to do more things and become more dependent on it.

But even that's not the big story here. The big story is that your world is going to change. What you think about and what you believe in will change. How you see the world will change. How you work will change, and how and what you buy will change. Moreover, your customers will change. How they think and what they buy will change. As a result, your business will need to change.

That's why it's imperative to think ahead and adopt new factory thinking. It will enable you to survive and succeed during the disruption caused by the singularity. It will empower you to build a new kind of business designed for the brave new world ahead of us.

To this end, I'll give you dozens of examples of how many companies—from large corporations to one-person home-based operations—have made the exciting transformation from old factory thinking to new factory thinking.

SECTION ONE

THE NEW FACTORY MARKETPLACE

CHAPTER 1

THE NEW MARKETPLACE REALITIES

Walking home from work one day, I bump into an old friend of mine. Her face is haggard, her shoulders are slumped, and tears roll down her cheeks.

"How's it going," I ask.

"Terrible," she says. "I got laid off from the bookstore."

"I'm so sorry to hear that," I commiserate, putting my hand on her shoulder. "What happened?"

"They laid off half the staff. They can't compete against online book retailers like Amazon. People don't buy as many books from us as they used to. They browse in the store and then order online."

"I know about that," I say. "They call that show-rooming. It's happening to lots of companies like retailers, travel agents, and insurance brokers. People spend time with a salesperson to pick their brain and then go online to get a deal."

"Well anyway," my friend says, moping up the tears on her face. "It cost me my job. And I don't know what I'm going to do."

I promise to keep her posted on any job openings I might hear about, but I'm not sure how to help her. I feel sad for my friend but I'm not surprised by her story. I hear tales like hers all the time. I have another friend who was unceremoniously escorted out of her office and turfed on to the street after doing a stellar job for 30 years. Her company had merged with a much larger firm and the new company trimmed its work force. "Nothing personal," they said, as a security guard asked her to turn over her laptop and cell phone.

The sad fact is: Lots of people are losing their old factory jobs and they have no vision for what to do next. Their only hope is that the economy will turn around, and companies will start hiring again. But that's not going to happen. The changes taking place in the marketplace are much bigger than any single job, company, business cycle or downturn. We're making the painful transition from the old factory marketplace to the new factory marketplace, and the best way to equip ourselves for the future is to recognize what's really going on, and embrace the new world that's emerging.

THE THREE FACTORS

Three factors are changing the marketplace on a fundamental level.

Factor #1: Exponential change: The pace of change is speeding up exponentially. In the past, market conditions changed slowly. Today, market conditions change much more quickly, usually with no advance warning.

Factor #2: Convergent competition: In the old factory marketplace, competition was constrained by trade barriers and controlled by industry regulations. In the new factory marketplace, companies have more competition converging on them from other countries and other industries. This convergent competition drives down prices and profit margins on traditional products and services.

Factor #3: Empowered prospects: In the new factory marketplace, communications technology empowers consumers to shop around for the lowest price if they think a product or service is a commodity. They also use technology to create a barrier between themselves and salespeople. This makes prospects harder to reach.

WHY THESE CHANGES ARE HAPPENING

The three factors of the new factory marketplace—exponential change, convergent competition, and empowered consumers—are caused by the ever-increasing processing power of computer-based devices and the expansion of the Internet. Previously, computers, the Internet and automated systems were simply tools to improve machine-based, old factory processes. But now, they have become the primary infrastructure of the global economy. This new "means of production" is having profound and irreversible repercussions in the marketplace. Clearly understanding these repercussions will empower you to deal with them effectively rather than being victimized by them.

THE REPERCUSSIONS

Repercussion 1: Conceptual Recombination

Every day, more people connect their computers, smart phones, tablets, and other devices to the Internet. Sensors, cameras and appliances are also being linked to the Internet, causing exponential growth in the number of connections on the network. In addition, computers and other devices are getting faster and more powerful.

This means more information is exchanged and processed every day.

This flood of information from multiple sources exposes people to novel concepts and ideas that they process and re-arrange in novel combinations. This "conceptual recombination" changes their worldview (their perceptions, beliefs, and preferences), and in effect, turns them into a new kind of person. It also turns them into a new kind of consumer, with different preferences about what they buy and how they buy.

Accelerated conceptual recombination also causes social, political and economic change. When people change their worldview (perceptions, beliefs, and preferences), they choose to live their lives differently (social), they demand different things from their leaders (political), and they change their behavior (economic). All of these changes alter market conditions.

In the old factory era, conceptual recombination was much slower. Because society was structured as a hierarchy, the elites at the top of the hierarchy tried to control what was communicated to the masses. In this environment, people's values, beliefs, and preferences changed slowly. As such, market conditions also changed slowly. In the new factory era, the emergence of non-hierarchical peer-to-peer communication is accelerating conceptual recombination and causing market conditions to change more quickly in unpredictable ways.

Repercussion 2: The Race To The Bottom

Increased global competition and the growing primacy of the Internet marketplace have turned most traditional products and services into commodities. A product or service becomes a commodity when buyers think all the suppliers in an industry or product category sell basically the same thing. When this happens, consumers look for the supplier with the lowest price. In this competitive environment, companies are forced to lower their prices. This race to the bottom is wonderful for consumers, but a challenge for producers. To stay competitive and maintain their profit margin, producers must cut costs. They cut costs in the following ways:

Lower cost of operations: Cut cost of labor. Replace people with computers, automation software, and robots. Get rid of physical assets like stores, manufacturing facilities and office space. Get customers to do work previously done by the company. Farm out operations to other countries with lower labor costs.

Lower cost of sales: Eliminate or scale back sales force. Use automated selling systems. Get prospects to do the work previously done by a salesperson.

Decrease percentage of fixed costs: Turn fixed costs into variable costs. Eliminate full-time employees. Outsource to other companies.

Lower the cost of risk: Download operations with high risk to outside companies. Impose tighter regulations and compliance requirements on down-stream sales and service organizations.

Achieve larger economies of scale: To lower costs per transaction, old factory companies merge and consolidate into larger operations and then engage in further cost cutting.

The effect of these changes is often lamentable but also

inevitable. When consumers seek lower prices, companies are forced to cut costs. This race to the bottom will cause millions of people to lose their old factory jobs.

Repercussion 3: The End Of The Middle Market

The Internet has taught consumers to look for the lowest price on anything they perceive as a commodity, even things not sold on the Internet. That's why most old factories now find themselves in a commodity marketplace where the only point of differentiation is price. This commoditization has gutted the middle market. Companies that try to maintain their existing cost structure and profit margins cannot compete against lower-priced rivals.

This state of affairs cleaves the marketplace into two camps: the fast food market and the gourmet market. In the fast food market, buyers look for the lowest price. In the gourmet market, buyers pay a lot of money for something special. This doesn't mean that poor people buy fast food and rich people buy gourmet. Every person, depending on the marketplace they're in, behave accordingly. If they're in the fast food marketplace (i.e. shopping online for life insurance or driving around to save at the gas pump), they look for the cheapest price. If they find themselves in the gourmet marketplace, the same person may buy an expensive fur coat or take their spouse to dinner at a chic restaurant.

This is an important point. The disappearance of the middle market is not because we have social disparity between rich and poor (although that's also a problem), it's because consumers now have two minds—fast food and gourmet—and employ one or the other depending on what marketplace they happen to be in. In other words, if a person is in the fast food marketplace, they look for the cheapest price, and if they're in a gourmet marketplace, they are willing to buy something expensive. This psychological behavior is adroitly explained in the book *Situations Matter* by Sam Sommers. He says behavior is not innate in a person's character, but rather shaped by the situations they find themselves in.

The implications of this new market reality are significant. If your company is stuck in the middle market, you'll be driven out of business. If you try to compete in the fast food market, you'll have to do more transactions in order to maintain your existing overhead and you may need to compete against much better capitalized rivals. For most companies, the only opportunity is to enter the gourmet marketplace. (Note: Gourmet does not necessarily mean a luxury good, just something considered significantly superior to a commodity.)

Repercussion #4: The End Of The Salesperson

In the new factory marketplace, people are exposed to thousands of marketing messages everyday, and to deal with this flood of data, they block out certain types of messages; especially anything that sounds like a sales pitch. So, if you send a sales message by email, your prospects probably won't read it. If you call them, they probably won't answer the phone, and if you mail them a brochure, they'll probably throw it out. This reality has increased the cost of sales and made the traditional sales approach ineffective.

That's why we are witnessing the end of the traditional salesperson. Consumers know the cost of sales is built into the price of a product and producers know the cost of sales is subtracted from their profit. For this reason, consumers have a financial incentive to do many traditional sales functions themselves (like searching for options and filling out forms), while producers are motivated to replace salespeople with computers and robots. That's why traditional salespeople who merely facilitate a transaction will become extinct.

This trend is already evident in sales-oriented professions like real estate, life insurance, and wholesaling. There's stiff commission competition in these industries. One of my clients, a real estate broker, cut his commission by 50%. Because he works at home and has low overhead, he could under-cut his competition and still make a good profit. His competitors (other real estate brokers) were furious (you can't do that, they said), but my client didn't care. He quickly got ten listings, made the sales, and pocketed a goodly sum. That's why some real estate brokers now offer zero commission in exchange for a flat fee. The same is happening in life insurance. In the U.K. and Australia, regulators eliminated commissions on life insurance. When that happened, many advisors left the industry because they couldn't figure out how to charge for their advice. That's why in the new factory era we'll see the end of the traditional salesperson.

Repercussion 5: The End of The Single Transaction

Because prospects are hard to reach, the cost of sales has gone up. It's now necessary to contact more prospects in order to land a sale. In some old factory industries, you also have more regulatory paper work. That's why you don't want to do a single transaction. Once you have a relationship with a customer, you want to sell them lots of things in order to cover the initial cost of acquiring them. That's why new factories that amortize the cost of customer acquisition over many years and many transactions out-compete old factories that only do single transactions.

Repercussion 6: The Freebie Factor

In the fast food marketplace, consumers look for the best price, and the best price is free. That's another thing the Internet has done to the brain of the consumer. They expect most things on the Internet to be free. This is a big danger for old factories because one of their competitors might start giving away their product or service for free in order to capture and own the relationship with the customer. One of my clients, a tax preparer, was compelled to build her new factory after a local insurance company started giving away free tax return services. "How can I compete if they give my service away for free?" she asked. Exactly. How can you? This highly disruptive trend will continue. More and more, commodity products and services will be given away for free by new factories intent on building their membership roster. I predicted this trend back in 1996 in my book *Strategic Marketing For The Digital Age*, and have watched it unfold ever since. (Also see Chris Anderson's book *Free: The Future of A Radical Price*).

Repercussion 7: The Demand For New Kinds Of Value

In developed economies most consumers have achieved physical actualization, meaning that most of their physical needs are being met. Of course, there are still many marginalized people, but even they are relatively better off than most people in the Third World. In this kind of mature marketplace, catering to a customer's physical needs is less of an opportunity than it used to be. For example, after World War Two, my father-in-law was the first person in his community to buy a refrigerator. Dozens of his friends came over to see the new invention. They had a refrigerator party. But today, everyone has a refrigerator. It's no big deal. Refrigerators have become a commodity; an essential one, but not something to throw a party about. And that's the thing. Back then, if you peddled refrigerators you sold something people got excited about and few people had. You also had few competitors so you could charge a good margin and make a good income. But nowadays, if you sell refrigerators, everyone has one, and there are a lot of people selling them. Customers can also go online and buy one themselves for dirt cheap and never talk to a salesperson.

That's the problem. If you only sell something tangible like a refrigerator, there's not a lot of opportunity to get rich in the new factory era. But that doesn't mean there is no opportunity. Once people get their physical needs met, there are other things you can help them with. This is where the opportunity lies: to package and sell new kinds of value that transcend the value provided by old factories. For example, the demand for emotional value will grow in the new factory marketplace. Once they have their physical needs met, consumers will be willing to pay a lot of money to feel better emotionally (i.e. feel less stressed, have more peace of mind, feel empowered, feel fulfilled, feel connected).

In the new factory marketplace, value will be created in ways that were previously unimaginable. Value will be created with "words" and "design" and other intangibles. New factories will transform the lives of their customers in holistic, integrated ways that are significantly superior to the fragmented approach taken by old factories. Opening our minds to the potential for new kinds of value is one of the keys to new factory thinking.

Repercussion 8: The End Of Fixed Overhead

In the new factory marketplace, companies will eliminate as much fixed overhead as possible. They will not want to commit resources to any physical or human asset that is "fixed" because they won't be sure if they'll need it in the future. In the old factory era, companies could confidently make a big fixed investment in overhead. They could invest $10 million in an assembly line to make hammers, and amortize that investment over 10 years. But in the new factory era, it's foolish to do that. There's no guarantee people will want hammers in 10 years or even one year from now. So new factories will avoid anything that fixes their overhead.

I had an experience that taught me this new factory lesson. Years ago, my company produced printed educational booklets for our clients. We generated $8,000 in revenue per month, incurring $4,000 in outside printing costs. Given the popularity of the booklets, we committed to lease a photocopier for $800 a month, thereby saving $3,200 a month in printing costs. It seemed like a good idea at the time, but it wasn't. A year later, no one wanted the printed booklets anymore. They wanted e-books. But we were left with six more years on the lease at $800 a month. The lesson was: while the photocopier was part of our fixed overhead, the demand for our product turned out to be variable. More excruciating (as all good lessons are), the photocopier spent the last two years of the lease in storage, and the total loss on the whole project amounted to about $30,000.

That's why fixed overhead is anathema in the new factory marketplace. New factories seek flexible overhead to match the malleability of the market. That's why my company now uses a nearby UPS store for our photocopier needs. If a client wants a printed booklet (sometimes they still do), we use the UPS machine and mark up the price. In this way, we turned a fix overhead cost into a variable cost, and always make money on a project.

In the new factory marketplace look for companies to shear off as much fixed overhead as they can; buildings, vehicles, machines, and of course, the biggest fixed overhead of them all, people. Companies will be forced to either hire people on contract or use outside suppliers. They will have little incentive to hire someone for a job, or to incur the additional fixed overhead associated with being an employer (such as desks, chairs, computers, phones, lunch rooms, toilet paper, insurance, and benefits).

Please don't misunderstand me. I'm not saying this is a good thing. I don't want to see people lose their jobs. It's just that the new factory marketplace forces companies to take these steps, even if they don't want to. To compete, they have to lower their fixed costs. They have to convert fixed costs into variable costs or go out of business. For these reasons, the ideal new factory will have virtually no fixed costs at all. It will be completely virtual.

Repercussion 9: No More Jobs

As flexible overhead replaces fixed overhead, millions of old factory jobs will be eliminated. Say good-bye to job security, defined benefits, and long-term employment. Lots of people will be replaced by computers and robots, or their old factory company will shut its doors. These displaced people will either spend the rest of their life unemployed or they will find work in the value hub economy. But notice I didn't say find a *job*, I said find *work*. This is a key distinction. In the new factory future, there won't be a lot of jobs, but there will be unlimited opportunities for work. As the value hub economy takes hold, an infinity of opportunities to provide value and make money will emerge, but not in the form of a traditional job. Jobs lost in old factories will not be replaced by jobs in new factories. Instead, everyone will act as a value hub connected to a network of other value hubs.

Repercussion 10: The End Of Industries

In the new factory marketplace, traditional industry definitions and structures are irrelevant. Ask yourself: what industry is Apple in? Is it in the computer industry or the telephone industry? What about Amazon? Is it in the book industry or the retail industry or the grocery industry?

The idea of industry silos and territories are of no interest to a new factory thinker. They cross over into any industry they want. Industry overlords, who have a vested interest in maintaining old factory perks and entitlements will of course, resist this trend. But it's all over for them because new factory consumers don't care what industry a company belongs to as long as it provides value.

As I write this, an internecine turf war is raging between Uber and the traditional taxi industry. Consumers love the improved value provided by Uber, but the traditional taxi industry is growling and biting back. This tug of war between new factory upstarts and industry-entitled old factories will be one of the most interesting dramas to play out in the new factory marketplace.

To succeed in today's marketplace, it's critical to get your head out of your industry-defined box. It's holding you back from seeing all of the potential value you could provide to your customers. Like Apple selling music, maybe you could sell your customers something from another industry or product/service category.

THESE CHANGES ARE IRREVERSIBLE

These changes and repercussions are unprecedented in human history. While they are caused by technology, they are not all about technology. It's about how people in the new factory marketplace see the world differently and behave differently in it. No amount of wishful thinking will reverse these trends. They're now firmly entrenched. The only path forward is to embrace the reality and the opportunities of the new factory marketplace. Now let's look at the difference between an old factory thinker and a new factory thinker.

CHAPTER 2

HARRY: AN OLD FACTORY THINKER

Millions of smart and hardworking people today have the ability to create a successful business. There's only one problem. They will probably use old factory thinking and that will doom their company right from the start.

To illustrate my point, consider Harry, one of those smart and hardworking people. During his spare time, Harry invents a new kind of hammer. It's three times lighter and 10 times stronger than other hammers on the market. Everyone agrees: it's a great hammer.

With encouragement from family and friends, he launches a company called Harry's Hammers. He leases industrial space and builds an assembly line to make hammers. He also hires employees and puts together a sales campaign.

After 18 months of preparation, Harry's sales team enters the marketplace. They have two targets: retailers and consumers. They want stores to stock their hammers, but they also plan to sell directly to consumers. After two weeks, a pattern emerges. The sales team reports that retail buyers are hard to reach. Almost every time they call a prospect, they get voice mail and have to leave a message. None of the prospects call back. So they call again and leave a second voice message along with an e-mail. But once again, the prospects don't respond. "It's kind of rude," one of the younger salespeople remarks.

The direct-to-consumer salespeople are also frustrated. They make 1,000 calls and only speak to 81 prospects. From that group, four purchase a hammer. The door-to-door salespeople are even more discouraged. They knocked on 450 doors, spoke to 33 prospects, and only sold two hammers. "To top it off," one of the salespeople reports, "I almost got bitten by someone's dog."

During the following months, the sales team keeps at it, and there are some encouraging developments. Two local retailers stock the hammers on a consignment basis (meaning they can return the hammers to Harry if they don't sell). As well, Harry sells 121 hammers online, although it's pointed out that the cost of online advertising strips away most of the profit.

After a year, Harry is both worried *and* optimistic. He hasn't sold very many hammers but he's making inroads. People tell him to keep at it. "It usually takes a few years for a new company to make a profit," supporters tell him. "The key is to persevere."

So Harry perseveres. He finds investors and expands his sales team. He creates a second-generation hammer, making it even lighter and stronger. But then something happens that Harry had not expected (although in hindsight, he realizes it was inevitable.) A new competitor from Asia enters the marketplace. Their hammer, called The Whammer 9000, looks a lot like Harry's hammer. It's also light and strong and has a streamlined futuristic shape. But that isn't the biggest problem. The Whammer 9000 is 25 per cent cheaper than Harry's hammer.

Harry buys a Whammer 9000 and checks it out. He gets some comfort from the fact that the upstart hammer isn't as good as his hammer. "Our hammer is lighter and stronger," he tells everyone. "Sure their hammer is less expensive, but our hammer is better quality."

Selling quality, however, is tough. Prospects only have one question: "How much?" When a salesperson explains that Harry's Hammer is better quality, and therefore more expensive, the prospects are unmoved. "You say your hammer is better but the people from Whammer say their hammer is better too," the prospects say. "And their hammer is cheaper. So we're going to stock the Whammer. If you can get your price down to their price, maybe we'll take another look at your hammer."

Unfortunately, that's just the beginning of Harry's woes. Over the next year, six other new competitors enter the hammer market. All claim their hammer is the best and all offer a lower price than Harry. Reluctantly, Harry decides to lower his price, cutting into his already slim profit margin. But even that doesn't work because three of the competitors promptly lower their price even more.

Determined to figure a way out of this quagmire, Harry brings his employees and investors together for a meeting. After spelling out the situation, Harry asks for suggestions. Everyone has an opinion on what to do. Some suggest they lower their price even more and make operations more efficient. Others suggest they branch out into screwdrivers and other tools such as wrenches and saws. A few of the younger employees think the company should make better use of social media. "We need to tweet more," Harry's son says.

"I appreciate all of your comments and suggestions," Harry says. "But I think we need to stay the course. We've got 20,000 hammers in the warehouse. The name of the company is Harry's Hammers. We can't start selling screwdrivers. That would confuse people. We just need to try harder. We need to make more calls and send out more emails. We need to hone our message and convince customers that our hammers are the best quality and worth a few extra dollars."

Two months later, Harry learns a national chain of hardware stores is running a promotion. To attract new customers, they're giving away free hammers (the Whammer 9000s!). Shortly thereafter, Harry files for bankruptcy. All the employees are laid off and 20,000 hammers are sold at auction for 35 cents each. Dejected but not defeated, Harry returns to the workbench in his garage. He has an idea for a new and better can opener.

So the question is: Why did Harry fail? Was it because no one wanted his hammers? Was it because he didn't know how to run a business? Was it because he used the wrong marketing strategy? No, Harry failed because he used old factory thinking. He approached his business like it was the 19th Century, not the 21st Century. Like many business people, he used a mental roadmap that no longer works in today's market conditions. To understand what I mean, let's imagine in the next chapter what would happen if Harry used new factory thinking.

CHAPTER 3

HARRY: A NEW FACTORY THINKER

As we saw in the last chapter, Harry's company went belly up because he used old factory thinking. Now let's imagine a parallel universe where Harry uses new factory thinking instead. To begin, Harry chooses to make his new factory not about a product or service but about a specific type of customer, namely Do-It-Yourselfers (DIYers). These are people who like to do their own renovations. Harry knows there are millions of DIYers around the world, and they have money to spend.

Focused on DIYers, Harry develops a big idea. He brainstorms ways to help DIYers get better results using less money, time, and energy. Tossing around ideas with his team, they hit upon a seemingly radical concept. Why not help DIYers connect with each other in order to exchange ideas and resources? "We could even help them share tools with each other," someone suggests.

In the old factory universe, Harry would have squashed such an idea. He would have said: "We don't want people sharing their tools with each other. We want each of them to buy a hammer." But in the new factory universe, Harry sees a bigger picture. Yes, he thinks, that's a great idea. We'll become the value hub at the center of this exchange and make lots of money. Another person suggests that members could help each other with projects, either by providing tips, or by actually helping them build something: kind of like an old fashion barn raising. Great idea, Harry exclaims, feeling a wave of excitement rising in his chest. Over the next couple of hours, ideas for creating value come fast and furious.

Harry then plays around with a few names for his big idea, and eventually settles on *The Do-It-Together Club*. He registers DoItTogether.club as a domain name and creates a simple website to get started. His goal is to sign up 1,000 members in the first year. He also packages three program levels: basic (free), premium ($25 a year), and super-elite ($150 a year).

When they sign up, members receive a lot of value. Using The Do-It-Together Club website (and later an app), members access a listing of the other members, find out what projects they're working on, and discover what tools they have to share (either free or for a rental fee). Members can also upload videos about a project they've done, like building a deck, or renovating a bathroom. The more videos they post, the more reward points they receive.

Harry finds that getting new members is easy. Signing up for membership is a no-brainer. It doesn't cost anything, and the club offers a lot of services even at the entry level. Within six months, Harry exceeds his 1,000-member target, and by the end of the first year, has 40,000 members. Harry is excited to see that membership growth is exponential. As more members join, the value of the club increases, attracting even more members.

After two years, Harry has 250,000 members in the network. Ninety percent are free members, 10 percent are paying members. He has 3,000 level two members at $25 a year ($75,000) and 1,000 level three members at $150 a year ($150,000) for a total membership revenue of $225,000. These are not big numbers, but Harry doesn't care. He's just getting started.

Building a roster of members is just part of the new factory game Harry is playing. He also makes money from his one-stop store where members purchase products and services at a discount. The first product added is of course Harry's Hammer. But Harry doesn't stop there. He adds The Whammer 9000, which in the old factory universe Harry would have never done. Then he adds screwdrivers, wrenches, saws, nails, lumber, drills and ultimately 10,000 other products. Of course, Harry doesn't make these products. That would be so old factory. No, Harry makes a deal with each supplier. They agree to give his members a discount, and give him 15% on every product sold. They agree to this commission because they seek access to Harry's growing roster of members.

Sales in the store keep growing. In the second year, total commission revenue is $600,000. Not a lot perhaps, but Harry keeps in mind that it's all high-profit revenue, with little or no risk attached. Harry is delighted to sell products created by other companies. He doesn't have to invest capital in factories, warehouses, and other infrastructure. He also doesn't need to worry about what products sell. If people stop buying hammers and start purchasing screwdrivers that will be just fine with Harry. He makes money either way. As Harry is fond of saying: Whether I sell a hammer or a screwdriver, the money looks the same in the bank.

Harry loves other things about his new factory. He doesn't have a lot of fixed overhead or operations. There are no machines to repair or light bulbs to replace. There are no carpets to clean or office supplies to buy. He also has more flexibility. He can run The Do-It-Together Club from anywhere. He spent three months last winter working from a beach house in the Caribbean, and this summer, he's heading to Italy to work there. All he needs is his laptop and a good Internet connection.

Harry also has a different perspective on creating equity in his business. In the new factory universe, Harry knows the value of his company grows as his network of members expands. The more members he has, the more his company is worth. He also knows that revenue growth is more predictable (revenue grows as memberships increase), and more consistent (83% of members renew their membership each year).

As a new factory thinker, Harry is always brainstorming about new ways to provide value to members. (*Thinking* has replaced *doing* as the primary value creation activity in the company.) In addition to home-building-related ideas, Harry plans to introduce other exchange-related concepts, such as home exchanges, car exchanges, baby-sitter exchanges, elder care help exchanges, and even a clothes exchange.

As he delves deeper into new factory thinking, Harry clearly understands that his company is now built around knowledge and relationships, not just the sales of tangible products and services. The benefit his company provides is embodied in a single word "empowerment". Anything that empowers members is something we could do, he tells himself. He also knows that his company's key solution is to facilitate an "exchange". Anything that helps our members make an exchange is also something we could do, he says. Taken together, Harry's business is now built around a simple phrase: *Empowerment Through Exchange.* With this in mind, Harry now has no barriers to his creativity, his intellectual interests, or his pathway to success. He's not limited in his thinking like old factory Harry. He's liberated to achieve his full potential.

Not surprisingly, Harry has many detractors when he veers off from his singular focus on hammers. "You're getting off track, Harry," a management consultant tells him. "You need to try harder to sell hammers, not get into this weird club thing." But Harry realizes the naysayers are mired in old factory thinking. They look at the world through 19th Century eyes, and don't appreciate how much the marketplace had changed. So he listens politely to their concerns and proceeds to build his new factory anyway. After all, he doesn't actually give up his old factory. He keeps selling hammers. In fact, in his third year running The Do-It-Together Club, he sells a record number of Harry's Hammers, along with an equal number of Whammer 9000s. Not to mention screwdrivers, drills, lumber, and hundreds of other products.

So the question is: What universe do you want to live in? The old factory universe or the new factory universe? I'm hoping you want to build a new factory. Bear in mind that Harry's situation might be different from your own. Harry had a product manufacturing company. You might run a service business, or sell to the consumer market or to businesses. You might work in a corporation, or a government agency. It doesn't matter. The principles of new factory thinking are universal. That's what makes new factory thinking so powerful. It's a universal model everyone can use. But before I show you how, let's look at the old factory business model in more detail.

BILL BISHOP

CHAPTER 4

THE OLD FACTORY MODEL

When Henry Ford perfected the moving assembly line in 1913, he ushered in the modern age. Old factory thinking had reached its zenith. Up to that point, cars had been built one at a time by craftsmen, making them too pricey for the average person. Ford's assembly line changed all that. Model T Fords took only 93 minutes to assemble with a new one coming off the line every three minutes. This efficiency allowed Ford to drop the price from $825 in 1908 to $575 in 1913. Millions of people could now afford to buy his car. Even better, Ford was able to raise wages from $1.50 a day to $5.00 a day, making it easier for his own workers to buy a car as well.

The spectacular success of Ford's assembly line was an inspiration to other entrepreneurs. They studied what Ford was doing and tried to copy his methods in their business. Initially, Ford's assembly line process was directly applied to other manufactured products but eventually influenced service businesses like restaurants and insurance companies. It also became the organizational model for other sectors such as education, healthcare, and government services. All the assembly lines in the economy then joined together into a single, integrated assembly line. Success as a company and as an individual meant fitting into this linear system; to find your place in the machine. Whether you worked on an assembly line in a factory, taught high school, or worked at home as a housewife, your role in life was oriented around the organizing principle of the assembly line. This way of life then conditioned our minds to think of the world as an assembly line: to be an assembly line person using assembly line thinking.

Today, the vast majority of the world's people still think and act like it's 1913. And because the world has changed, they feel like strangers in a strange land. They don't know how to navigate this new landscape so they often feel frustrated, angry and scared. You might feel that way yourself. I know I did. That's why we need to deconstruct our old factory thinking. We have to make it visible and then do away with it.

So what does an assembly-line-oriented mind look like? Let's take a look at the underlying concept of an assembly line. It works like this:

1. Acquire resources from the environment or from other organizations.
2. Assemble these resources in an efficient step-by-step process.
3. Deliver a quality product or service at a low price.

When you get it right, an assembly line is an amazing thing. You can produce millions of cars, toasters, hamburgers, life insurance policies, and handbags, and do it in less time and for less money. You can lower your prices and attract more customers, and if you're a nice employer like Henry Ford, you can raise salaries and give your productive employees big bonuses.

The assembly line economy was a wonderful thing. It raised the standard of living for billions of people and created the modern economy we have today, but it came with an unexpected consequence. It wired our minds to see the world from an assembly line perspective. It told us to:

- Do more;
- Do things faster;
- Use more resources;
- Focus on producing and selling more products/services;
- Specialize in a product or service;
- Focus on your individual objective; and
- Measure results quantitatively.

Old factory thinking pervaded all areas of society but it became manifest most visibly in the structure of companies. Each company was designed as an assembly line, and endeavored to fit into the overall assembly line structure of the economy. Creating and operating a business meant creating and operating an assembly line. This led to a four-stage thinking process, which I call the old factory business model. The four stages are:

1. Pick a product or service
2. Set up operations
3. Make a sales pitch
4. Do transactions

1. Pick a product or service

Like Harry with his hammers, old factory thinkers begin with an idea for a product or service. Perhaps they want to design wedding dresses or become a cosmetics wholesaler. Or maybe they want to provide in-home eldercare services or host extreme travel in the arctic. Some of their ideas might be truly innovative and creative but they make a critical error. By defining their business around a particular product or service, they don't think about what will happen in the future when their offering no longer interests customers or when new competitors start selling the same thing. They don't take into account change or competition as inevitable factors. And because of this, they may one day regret being typecast.

The other problem with building a business around a product or service is that you unnecessarily restrict your potential. If you think you're in the hammer business, you don't contemplate selling screwdrivers. You lock yourself into a very narrow box. Theodore Levitt, a marketing professor at Harvard, diagnosed this self-limiting mentality in the 60s as "marketing myopia". He used the example of the railroad companies at the turn of the 20th Century who thought they were in the "railroad" business and didn't see the potential of branching out into automobiles, airplanes, and other transportation-related businesses. According to Levitt, this myopia caused the railroads to define themselves too narrowly, and as a result, they missed out on big opportunities for growth.

Having product or service ideas is not wrong. Keep coming up with ideas to provide new kinds of value. Just don't define yourself or your business based on these products or services.

2. Set up operations

With a product or service in mind, the old factory thinker then sets out to construct an operational structure to make and deliver it. This often begins with a desk, a computer, telephone, a pad of paper and a pen. This simple start can then lead to giant factories with multi-stage assembly lines, scores of employees punching the clock, and all of the other operational paraphernalia associated with a growing enterprise such as trucks, warehouses, signage, photocopiers, and insurance.

But this focus on expanding operations is a trap. Because old factory operations are designed around a particular product or service, you restrict your ability to adapt to changes in the marketplace. If you have an assembly line to make hammers, it's not easy to start making something else. You also turn a blind eye to the potential of other things because you're emotionally and financially invested in your infrastructure. In addition, the cost of operations turns into a huge problem if your product or service becomes a commodity. As the price of your product falls, the cost of your overhead remains the same (or increases) and this takes a big bite out of your profits.

3. Make sales pitch

Nothing epitomizes the old factory era more than the image of a door-to-door salesman peddling vacuum cleaners to apron-clad housewives in the 1950s. While the tacky glad-handing salesperson is a firmly-entrenched cultural icon that makes us chuckle, most companies today still engage in the same basic approach to sales. Once they've chosen their product or service, and built operations around it, they enter the marketplace and give a sales pitch: *Here is our great product. It's better than anything else on the market. It's got these amazing features. Here's the price. We'll give you a deal.*

In the old factory era, straight-up sales worked great. People were interested in hearing a sales pitch. They weren't being bombarded with thousands of sales messages a day. They were also more accessible because they couldn't hide behind technology like security systems and voice mail. If you knocked on their door, they would have probably answered it, and if you called them, they would have probably picked up the phone. But that's not the world we live in today. Prospects are much harder to reach because they abhor a sales pitch.

Besides being ineffective, a sales pitch mentality has other drawbacks. By focusing on the features and benefits of your product, you fail to investigate the true needs and wants of your customers. If you have a quota to sell 1,000 hammers this month, you won't ask the customer what they really want. You don't care. You don't want to discover they really want screwdrivers. You want them to buy hammers. This emphasis on your personal product (hammers) and your own goals (sell 1,000 hammers) can make you self-absorbed and uninterested in other people, and stop you from developing bigger relationships and making bigger sales.

4. Do transactions

The fourth step—do transactions—is the way old factory thinkers keep score of their success. If they sell 10,000 hammers this year, they want to sell 20,000 hammers next year. Pumping more products and services through the assembly line becomes the key driving force of the organization. All the intellectual and creative energy of the company is focused on determining one thing: how can we move more of our product? While this sounds like the right course of action, transaction-oriented goal-setting is another old factory trap because it diverts attention away from opportunities that might prove to be much more lucrative. By only thinking about how to sell hammers, you don't create other kinds of value (like screwdrivers) that might be even more profitable.

DECODING THE MACHINE LANGUAGE

This four-stage process is so engrained in our thinking we don't question it. But that's what I'm asking you to do: question it. Notice your own thought process. Is your business defined by its product or service? Are your operations built around that product or service? Do you make a sales pitch? Do you keep score by tracking transactions?

If you're honest, you'll admit you use old factory thinking. But don't worry. You're not alone. It's used by 99.9% of business people today, in every kind of business in every kind of industry. This includes manufacturers, service companies, wholesalers, and retailers. It applies equally to consumer or business-to-business-oriented companies. It also applies to most Internet-based enterprises.

The old factory business model is so ingrained in our thinking that we don't know it's there. It's like a computer's machine language. That's the deep code programmed into a computer's chip. Most people don't know about this level of programming in their computer. They're familiar with their computer's operating system (like iOS) and its individual software applications (such as Word or Excel), but they don't know about its machine language. And yet, it's the machine language that dictates the structure of the operating system and the software applications. The same is true with the old factory business model. It's been the core programming of all companies during the past 200 years but it's so engrained in our thinking that we don't even know it's there.

Now let's turn to the next chapter and discuss an alternative: The new factory model.

CHAPTER 5

THE NEW FACTORY MODEL

Harry was more successful when he used new factory thinking because it freed his mind from a limited self-definition—we are a hammer company. It enabled Harry to create new forms of value previously beyond his imagination and it gave him a new blueprint for building his business. This new factory structure has five elements:

1. Specialize in one type of customer
2. Help your customers achieve a big idea
3. Provide free value during the sales process
4. Enroll customers in a membership program
5. Sell products and services from a one-step store

1. Specialize in one type of customer

Unlike an old factory designed around a product or service, a new factory is designed around a single type of customer. As in the example given earlier, instead of building a business around "hammers" you build a business around "do-it-yourselfers". The new factory is then defined not by *what* it makes and sells; it's defined based on *whom* it helps.

This customer-first perspective unshackles your mind. You are now free to think of new ways to help your customers; ways that go beyond the standard products offered in your industry. In fact, you are free to make and sell anything as long as it's considered valuable by your customers. This realization keeps your mind curious, nimble and intellectually engaged.

From an operational standpoint, this opened-minded attitude means you begin each relationship with a blank slate and work through a discovery process to help your customers articulate their goals and then make a plan to achieve them. Based on what you are learning from the marketplace (i.e. people want screwdrivers, not hammers) you're prepared to restructure your entire business if it will better assist your customers in achieving their goals.

On a deeper level, building your business around a customer type helps you escape from an egocentric worldview. Instead of your business being all about you, your business is all about others. This is not only more meaningful, it's good for business. Using the new factory model helps you align your social good intentions with the dictates of making a living, something that the old factory model often made difficult.

Building your business around a type of customer, instead of products and services, also makes sense in a fast-changing marketplace. I've seen many people tie their reputation in the marketplace to a particular product or service only to find that its popularity was fleeting. Then they had to start again by re-branding themselves (usually around another product or service). This is a bad idea in a marketplace that is constantly changing. However, if you pick the right type of customer, you never have to change it no matter what happens in the marketplace. This gives your business a strong anchor of stability that's impervious to inevitable changes in market conditions.

2. Help your customers achieve a big idea

A big idea communicates what a new factory tries to help its customers achieve, and the unique way it helps them achieve it. It's not an idea for a product or service; it's an intangible concept. Customers don't hold it in their hands, they hold it in their minds. It has two key components: the *BIG Goal* and the *Signature Solution*.

The big goal is transcendent: it's a desired outcome that transcends the small-minded benefits achieved by old factories. It's also an intention rather than a promise. You can't guarantee you'll achieve it, but you have the intention to try. Here are a few examples of big goals:

- Be ten times safer
- Be ten times more fulfilled
- Be ten times more connected
- Have 20 times more fun
- Lower your costs by 50%
- Increase sales by 300%
- Make twice the income while working 50% less time
- Lose 100 pounds in six months
- Win a gold medal at the Olympics
- Feel greater well-being using less resources

To be effective, a big goal needs to be lofty and challenging. This gets customers to take notice and get inspired about what you're trying to do. You want your potential customers to see that you're trying to help them achieve something big and significant.

Another part of the big idea is the signature solution. This is a new, more advanced approach that helps your customer achieve the big goal. It's based on your years of experience working with many customers. Over that time, you've learned what works and what doesn't, and have boiled it down to one key action, tool or strategy. For example, to help someone lose 100 pounds in six months, you might have a signature solution called *The Hopping Method*. You teach your customers to hop on one leg for an hour a day, and by doing so; they lose the 100 pounds (as long as they don't drink six beers at the same time!). Over the years, you've learned that hopping is a good way to lose weight.

Packaging a big idea provides many benefits to a new factory thinker. One, it's easy to test in the marketplace. Without investing a lot of capital, you can try the idea on a few existing customers to see if it works. If it doesn't work then you can easily pivot to an alternative idea. In this way, you can quickly ascertain the best big idea. Secondly, it's another great anchor. No matter what happens in the marketplace, your big idea doesn't need to change. For example, its unlikely people in the future won't want to lose 100 pounds in six months. Thirdly, the big idea refocuses your intellectual and creative energies. Instead of trying to figure out how to sell more products, you now focus on thinking about new ways to help your customers achieve their goals. Having a more transcendent intention, that's all about your customers, not about you, opens the closed fist of your mind.

3. Provide free value during the sales process

In order to draw prospects out of their sales-pitch bunker, new factory thinkers provide free value during the sales process. It's like giving away a free piece of chocolate in order to sell the whole box.

The immediate objective of the free value strategy is to sign up *subscribers*. You nail down a formal relationship with a prospect by getting them to sign up for a mailing list or a free service. This technique is now commonplace. Many companies offer prospects a free version of their service, either for a month, or on an on-going basis. For example, Skype provides subscribers with free telephone service. Google provides dozens of free applications, and Apple provides thousands of free apps. Their objective is to get lots of free subscribers and then convert them into paying members.

By becoming a subscriber, the person is required to give a certain amount of personal information and agree to receive some form of on-going communication. This is called *permission marketing*, a term coined by Seth Godin in his book of the same title. Eventually some of the subscribers move to the next level and become a member.

Giving free value during the sales process can take many forms. It can be a subscription to an e-mail newsletter or a free version of your product or service. It can be a certain amount of consulting time. Ideally, the free value is a facsimile or segment of the membership program (see next step) so the subscriber gets a taste of what they will experience if they become a full-fledged paying member.

The free value approach gives a new factory a huge advantage over its competitors who use traditional sales techniques. One, it's much easier to attract a prospect when you give them something for free. You don't have to spend time selling; you just give them the free sample. This speeds up the sales process and lowers your cost of sales. Additionally, providing free value gives you more leverage in the company-prospect relationship. To get the free value, the prospect must give you something: either their personal information and/or their attention. You can also dictate who gets the free value and who doesn't. Like a bouncer at a popular nightclub, you decide who gets in and who doesn't. Psychologically, by restricting access to the free value, you increase its perceived value, making it even more desirable.

Most importantly, free value helps you bring more potential customers into your world. It creates a crowd around your business and projects an aura of popularity. It also gives you a much larger group of prospects to work with and enables you to demonstrate the value you provide, rather than just talk about it. It also enables you to shed the negative image of a salesperson and be perceived instead as someone who is successful, popular and in-demand.

4. Enroll customers in a membership program

A old factory has customers, a new factory has members. Because they are part of a "program" these members have "membership consciousness." They are conscious of being part of a larger community and feel a special affiliation with the new factory. And because they have received a lot of value from the new factory—both before and after becoming a member—they're open to buying other things, even if the products and services do not fall within the original industry-parameters of the relationship. (For example, people who originally bought a computer from Apple now purchase music, telephones and apps. Amazon customers who originally bought books now buy groceries, office supplies and fitness equipment.)

The most important marketing objective of a new factory is to sign up members. If it has 2,000 members this year, it wants 4,000 members next year. To get and keep these members, it sets up a structured program packaged with a range of membership benefits. It makes it clear what members get that non-members don't get. (That's why Amex says membership has its privileges). It either charges a fee for membership, or provides it for free, in the hopes of selling products from its one-stop store (see next).

Fostering membership consciousness is important because customers today are fickle. They don't feel guilty about shopping around for the best price or jumping ship to a competitor for a better deal. But members stay put because they are imbedded in the company's eco-system. For example, my stepdaughter Robin kept exhorting me to switch from an iPhone to an Android smart phone. "It's a better phone," she said. But I told her I couldn't do it even if I wanted to because I was ensconced in the Apple eco-system. "I would have to change my whole life if I switched from Apple to Android," I said.

The most powerful reason why members become firmly attached to a new factory is because they buy into its big idea. They have a powerful "why" in their mind about why they have a relationship with the new factory (i.e. becoming 10 times safer, more fulfilled or more connected), and they realize the new factory is the only company that provides the big idea. To go to another supplier is simply not an option, either practically or emotionally.

5. Sell products and services from a one-stop store

A new factory is not tied to any particular industry. While it's old factory may have started in a traditional industry, the new factory sells products and services from multiple industries. The best current example is Apple: it sells its traditional products from the computer industry, but also sells products from the music, telephone, and movie industries.

By expanding into other industries, and selling products created by other companies, the new factory expands its potential revenue without increasing its risk profile, capital investments or fixed overhead. By sourcing outside suppliers, it leverages existing resources in the economy. The suppliers are willing to give the new factory a commission or finder's fee because they don't have to do any marketing. They're willing to pay a premium in order to reach the ever-expanding roster of the new factory's membership. (That's why Apple is able to command a 30% fee for selling music, movies, and apps.)

By selling products and services produced by other companies, the new factory also takes advantage of the long tail strategy (see Chris Anderson's book *The Long Tail*). This means the new factory has a huge supply of products and yet doesn't need to worry which products sell and which don't. For example, Apple doesn't worry which song is a hit; it makes money no matter what. The same applies to Amazon. They don't care which book becomes a best-seller.

The one-stop store is a win-win for all three parties: the members, the suppliers and the new factory. The members win because they have a single place to get everything they need. The suppliers win because they gain access to previously-hard-to-reach prospects, and the new factory wins because it generates passive income. The overall economy also benefits because the new factory generates demand for previously under-utilized resources.

THE OPEN MIND

One of the biggest problems with old factory thinking is that it closes your mind to potential opportunities. It stops you from imagining new ways to help people. It makes you egocentric and turns your mind into a closed fist.

New factory thinking and the new factory model, however, open the closed fist of your mind. The very bones of your company embody a customer-first philosophy. It sets your sights much higher and brings into action your best intentions. It allows you to demonstrate to prospects the value you provide without turning them off with a sales pitch. It also honors the relationship you have with your best customers by designating them as members. And finally, it maximizes your revenue potential by providing your members with a vast compendium of resources in a one-stop store.

The new factory is also structured to match the new conditions of the 21st Century marketplace: exponential change, convergent competition, and empowered consumers. Designed as a value hub, the new factory connects its network of members to its network of suppliers, and grows organically by continuously expanding the size of both networks. It adapts easily to changes in the marketplace because its core business anchors—its customer type and big idea—

are future-proof. Operating within this model, the new factory is able to continuously expand its influence, its customer relationships, and its value propositions. That's why companies designed as new factories will proliferate and prosper in the coming years while companies designed as old factories will falter and vanish.

Now let's turn to a detailed look at each of these five elements in the next section: *Building Your New Factory*.

SECTION TWO

BUILDING YOUR NEW FACTORY

CHAPTER 6

STEP 1: ONE CUSTOMER TYPE

"The best thing I ever did was specialize in working with the owners of construction companies," Doug, a life insurance salesman, told me. "That strategy made all the difference."

When I first met Doug he was frustrated about his business. "My prospects think I'm just another guy who sells life insurance and I don't know how to explain why they should work with me instead of someone else. Life insurance is a commodity. You can get it anywhere."

To deal with his problem, Doug began with step 1 of the new factory thinking process: *Specialize in one type of customer.* After some consideration, Doug decided to focus on the owners of construction companies. He already had a few of them as clients and they had proven to be profitable and enjoyable people to work with.

Fast-forward ten years. Doug had signed up more than 100 members in his program. Each member was an owner of a construction company and most of them bought large life insurance policies. Doug had made a bundle and was now ready to retire. He said: "The most important thing I ever did was specialize in one type of customer. When I told the owners of construction companies that I specialized in them, they loved it. It gave them a reason to pick me over another life insurance agent who wasn't a specialist."

There are many good reasons to specialize in one kind of customer. One, it takes the focus off your needs and your goals, and puts the emphasis where it belongs: on the needs and goals of your customers. Secondly, it makes your business more focused and easier to run. With one type of customer, you only need one system to take care of them. You can continuously improve this single system, rather than tinker with multiple systems. Third, it releases you from the confines of your industry and product/service category. Because your business is all about helping a certain type of person, you now have permission to do anything to help them, even things that currently fall outside the normal parameters of your industry.

When you use old factory thinking, your imagination rarely ventures beyond the value boundaries of your industry. But when you build your business around a type of customer—instead of a product or service—there are no barriers to what you can do.

To choose your customer type, review your current list of customers. Identify the best ones. Who do you like best? Do they fit within any definable segment? Are they women or fitness buffs? Are they nurses or teachers? Are they young families or retirees, or another definable market segment?

Here are some real world companies that are built around a customer type, not a product or service.

The Running Room: This Canadian company is a value hub for runners.

Allnurses: Their website provides nurses with educational, networking, and career services.

Firehouse: They provide a full range of products and services to firefighters.

Lefty's: The Left Hand Store: They provide products designed for left-handed people.

All About Birds: This organization caters to bird watchers.

Tall Friends: If you're tall and looking for a tall mate, visit tallfriends.com

Solo Traveller: Blogger Janice Waugh has established herself as the go-to expert for people who like to travel on their own. Visit solotravelerblog.com

Just Multiples: This company caters to parents of twins and triplets.

Just For Red Heads: If you're a redheaded female, they have beauty products just for you.

Action Plan

1. Review your list of customers and identify the best ones.

2. Based on your list, pick your customer type.

3. Tell people you specialize in a particular type of person or organization.

Note about action steps: At the end of each chapter in this section, I give you action steps. You can start implementing these concepts right away. You don't need to wait until you finish the book. See *The Lean Startup* by Eric Ries for more guidance on this approach.

CHAPTER 7

STEP 2.1: THE BIG GOAL

"We choose to go to the moon in this decade and do the other things, not because they are easy, but because they are hard."
President John F. Kennedy, September 12, 1962

President Kennedy was a new factory thinker. He understood the power of big ideas. He knew big ideas inspire and motivate people to achieve incredible things.

That's what you can do: Use a big idea to marshal all of your talents, knowledge and energy to achieve really big things. There's only one catch. You will help other people achieve those really big things, not yourself.

A big idea has three parts: the big goal, the big problem, and the signature solution. A big goal is what you try to help people achieve, the big problem is what's stopping them from achieving the big goal, and the signature solution is the unique way you help people overcome the big problem and achieve the big goal. We'll cover the big goal in this chapter, and the big problem and the signature solution in the next two.

A big goal is about your customers, not about you

This is the most important principle. Old factory thinkers strive to achieve their own goals. New factory thinkers make it their intention to help other people achieve *their* goals.

For instance, an athletic coach can try to help athletes win a gold medal at the Olympics. A doctor can try to help her patients be 20 times healthier. And someone in the entertainment business can try to help his customers have 50 times more fun.

A big goal motivates new factory thinkers to create new kinds of value. For instance, the coach might create an advanced training process to help athletes overcome their psychological roadblocks to higher performance. The doctor might develop an holistic healthcare model that combines acupuncture, yoga and mindfulness meditation. And the entertainment entrepreneur might develop a new kind of hologram-based adventure game using augmented reality.

The important thing is to make the goal really big. No one will get inspired if you try to help them improve productivity by 9 percent or lose 15 pounds in eight months. Those goals are too small. Try to help them increase productivity by 300% or lose 100 pounds in six weeks. That's big.

Thinking small won't get anybody excited—including you. But thinking big, and telling people about your big goal for them, will draw more people into your orbit. It doesn't matter if people say your ambitions are too big, they'll be thinking and talking about you nonetheless.

So stretch yourself. Don't listen to skeptics who say it can't be done. Who cares about them? Thinking big will attract the kind of big-thinking customers you want to work with. That's why I admire entrepreneurs with super-size ambitions who aren't shy about making them public. Thinking big is the reason why they get so much free publicity in the media. People are interested in what they're trying to do and respect them for their ambitions.

When you set the big goal, don't worry about how you're going to do it. Just give yourself permission to think big. But once again remember: This is a big goal for your customers, not you. An old factory thinker might set a goal to be 10 times richer. A new factory thinker would set a goal to make her customers 10 times richer.

I don't want to gloss over this point too quickly because it's a critical component of new factory thinking. The old factory era conditioned us to focus on our own personal goals, not the goals of others. But in the new factory marketplace, nobody cares about your goals. They want to know what you can do for them.

In today's marketplace, especially in the western world, most people have achieved a lot of goals already. They have a house and a car and enough food to eat. They have televisions, computers, and smart phones. Lots and lots of stuff. So what's next? What are new goals that go above and beyond the goals they have already achieved?

A big goal will give your customers something new to want and aspire to. While there's a place in the new factory process to ask customers what they currently want and need, it's more advanced to give them an idea for a new goal; something they haven't thought about before. A member of my coaching program, for example, tries to help his clients have 100 times more peace of mind about their financial affairs. Another entrepreneur I work with has made it his big goal to help manufacturers optimize their industrial design process. Another of my members—a life coach—tries to help people enhance their feelings of self-worth by 25 times.

The point is: These new factory thinkers don't let their customers decide what the goal is. No, they suggest bigger and better goals for the customer to pursue. For instance, in the 1990s, a life insurance company in Canada ran television ads about young-looking 55-year-olds enjoying their retirement. The narrator explained that you no longer needed to wait until 65 to retire; you could retire at 55 instead.

The ads were a sensation. With the retire-at-55 idea planted in their mind, a lot of prospects contacted the company. "I want to retire at 55," they said. The campaign was so successful the company changed its name to Freedom 55 Financial.

So new factory thinkers challenge their customers to think bigger and better. They accept the fact that their customers are usually caught up in their own limited thinking about what's possible. As Henry Ford commented: "If I had asked my customers what they wanted, they would have said: faster horses." (This concept of challenging your customers to think bigger is explained very well in a book called *The Challenger Sale* by Matthew Dixon and Brent Adamson.)

When you set your big goal, you'll notice an instantaneous increase in your energy and focus. You'll start "imagineering" new ways to help your customers achieve it. If your big goal is to help people cut their home energy consumption by 10 times, you'll become obsessed about it. You'll do research. You'll experiment with new technologies. And you'll bring in other experts and strategic partners. You'll become increasingly smarter and more knowledgeable about how to accomplish the big goal.

My intention is to help you become 100 times more successful and fulfilled, and by extension make the world economy 100 times more prosperous. It's a tall order, but I'm energized by it. It gives me a focus for learning and thinking. I don't sit around complaining about the state of the world. I take action to make the world a better place.

I used to be solely focused on my own personal goals. But I learned that helping other people achieve their goals is the best way for me to achieve my own goals. It also makes me feel better. I feel more connected to the world, and my work has greater meaning for me.

Imagine what would happen if everyone went to work each day with the intention of helping others achieve big goals. What do you think would happen? I believe the economy would soar. Everyone would be an ardent value creator. They would use more of their brain power and creativity. They would feel better about themselves. And they would employ more of their skills, talents and knowledge.

So set a big goal. Help others achieve it.

Action Plan

1. Think about your customers. What goals have they already achieved? What new, bigger goals could you help them accomplish? (Remember: Make the goals about them, not about you.)

2. From your list, choose the big goal you're most excited about. Tell people about it. (Note: Remember that your big goal is an intention, not a promise.)

3. Think about the things you already do to help your customers achieve the big goal. Then think about new knowledge, resources, and tools to enhance your existing capabilities. Identify outside partners who can also help your customers achieve the big goal.

Of course you don't know how to do it

The key reason why most people never set a big goal, even for themselves, is because they immediately say they don't know how to accomplish it. But that's not what new factory thinkers do. They admit they don't know how to do it and then they try to figure it out. After all, did America know how to land a man on the moon when Kennedy made his famous speech? No. But they figured it out. You can do the same thing.

CHAPTER 8

STEP 2.2: THE BIG PROBLEM

I saw a billboard on the highway that read: "Do you have toe-nail fungus?" I had never heard of the affliction, and didn't think I had it, but a little bit of doubt crept into my mind. Maybe I have toenail fungus and don't know it, I thought. That evening I checked my toes. They looked good, surely no fungus. But just to be on the safe side, I bought the toe-nail fungus ointment. How about you? Do you have toenail fungus?

Bringing previously unknown and undiagnosed problems to the attention of customers is a tried-and-true marketing method used by advertising agencies for decades. The strategy is to get people worried about something they don't know they should be worried about and then offer them a cure. This strategy can be used unethically to sell snake oil and other bogus remedies, but it's also an important step in the development of legitimate big ideas that can truly help people in significant ways.

That's why new factory thinkers look for big problems to solve. They look for inefficiencies, fragmentation, unmet needs, and unnecessary suffering and then get to work creating innovative solutions to these problems.

In 1999, I wrote a book called *The Strategic Enterprise* in which I put forward a problem I called *The Product-First Trap*. I had asked myself: "What is the core reason why companies get stuck in low growth?" and I realized it was because they become fixated on their products and can't see other opportunities to create value for their customers.

After the book was published, I spoke at the annual sales conference for Johnson & Johnson, the consumer products and pharmaceutical company. Speaking before a group of 200 executives, I outlined the symptoms and repercussions of *The Product-First Trap*. Ten minutes into my talk, the CEO stood up and said: "Bill is right, we're caught in the product-first trap. We need to listen carefully to what he has to say and get out of this trap." Needless to say, the rest of the talk went very well and I landed a sizeable consulting contract.

I had a similar experience five years previously following the release of my book about Internet marketing called *Strategic Marketing For The Digital Age*. In the book I diagnosed a problem called *Technopia*. When companies have this problem they become overly obsessed with technology and ignore fundamental business and marketing principles. In my estimation, I believed people had been entranced by Internet hysteria. I was vindicated for my conviction in 1999 when the .com bubble burst.

Coining the phrase *Technopia* proved to be a lucrative strategy. One morning in mid-December 1997, I got a call from the vice-president of marketing at IBM. He had read my book and was convinced that IBM had a virulent case of *Technopia*. He wanted to hire me to cure the problem. Amusingly, he asked me to come over right away to pick up a check for $50,000 so he could include it in his department's expenditures for the current budget year. As you can imagine, I did not hesitate to oblige him.

Old factory thinkers often start off as problem solvers (e.g. people need shoes or life insurance) but eventually they stop trying to solve their customers' problems and focus exclusively on trying to sell their products. New factory thinkers, on the other hand, spend the majority of their time thinking about their customers' problems. New factory thinkers look for patterns of pain that their customers can't see. This wide-view pattern recognition gives new factory thinkers the ability to identify problems that are constraining, if not killing, their customers.

Certainly there is no shortage of problems. Whether we're talking about a person, a company, or society in general, there are endless problems to solve. Take a close look and you'll see problems everywhere. You might see that companies are wasting energy in their manufacturing process. You might notice that too many people suffer from obesity because they eat too much fast food. Or you might ascertain that there is a high level of adult illiteracy in your community.

Bear in mind that you don't have to solve the big problem all on your own. Rather, you act as a "value hub" and integrate different resources to solve the issue. In their excellent book *The Solution Revolution*, authors William D. Eggers and Paul Macmillan, give dozens of examples of companies and social entrepreneurs who have successfully tackled big problems. For example, the people at Unilever made it their objective to solve the problem of deaths from diarrhea in developing countries by bringing together a team of players including governments, NGOs, and community entrepreneurs. Using innovative strategies they developed and marketed a new brand of soap that was affordable to people who earn less than $1 a day. By first identifying a big problem, Unilever now makes big monetary profits while achieving an important social outcome (lower deaths from diarrhea).

In another case, a social entrepreneur in China has built a thriving business making clothing out of plastic retrieved from the ocean. She started the company after learning about all the plastic waste accumulating in the ocean. She asked herself: How can we clean up this plastic problem and make money at the same time? This led to the idea of paying fishermen to retrieve the detritus from the ocean and then to make clothes out of the recycled plastic.

Giving the problem a name, like toenail fungus, is very effective. It helps your customers get their head around the idea. For example, Fabreze created a series of humorous online commercials to introduce a problem they call *noseblindness*. When you have this disorder, you are unable smell the unpleasant odors in your house. Left untreated, this affliction can cause embarrassment when friends and family, who are not noseblind, come over to visit.

Noseblindness is a brilliant example of a big problem because it raises doubt in the mind of the customer. When they hear about this new disease, they wonder: "Does my house smell and I don't know it? Am I noseblind?" Once this doubt is planted in their mind, the only apparent answer is to spray everything in your house with Fabreze—just in case.

To pinpoint the big problem, look beyond symptoms. Figure out what's causing the symptoms. It might be something the customer is doing (i.e. lung cancer caused by smoking two packs a day) or something they're not doing (i.e. falling profits caused by unproductive employees). The big problem can also be an erroneous way of thinking. Consider the captain of the Titanic. He thought— erroneously—that he had an unsinkable ship. This stopped him from taking necessary precautions—such as looking out for icebergs and getting more lifeboats. Helping him change his thinking could have saved many lives, including his own.

In this book, the problem I diagnose is old factory thinking. It's not just that companies are solely focused on their products (the product-first trap) it's that they use an outdated thinking process in a new kind of marketplace. Left untreated, this problem can and does cause companies to stagnate, and in many cases, go out of business.

Look for problems and the reasons for the problems. Why are companies not growing? Why are people unhealthy? Why are so many kids dropping out of school?

When you engage in this kind of new factory thinking, you move beyond cynicism and resignation. You realize being a problem-solver is better than being a complainer. What does complaining do for you anyway? Does it ever solve a problem? No. It just makes you depressed and angry.

So stop complaining and start problem solving. Identify a big problem and make it your mission to solve it. Don't be put off by complainers and cynics. Find positive people who want to help you solve the big problem.

By addressing a big problem, new parts of your brain are activated and your intellectual battery is recharged. You feel more positive and engaged in your life and your work. You also attract and influence other problem-solvers to join you in your mission.

So what's the big problem you want to solve?

Action Plan

1. Think about your customers. What are the big problems they have that are not being addressed by old factories? Why do they have these big problems? What are they doing wrong, or not doing, that is causing these problems? Are they being held back by an outdated or unhelpful way of thinking? If so, what is this outdated or unhelpful way of thinking?

2. From your list, choose the big problem that you want to tackle. Choose the big problem that gives you a feeling of energy and purpose.

3. Give the big problem a name like *toe-nail fungus* or *noseblindness.*

4. Tell people about the big problem. Tell them you're actively solving this problem. Get them to help you with it.

CHAPTER 9

STEP 2.3: THE SIGNATURE SOLUTION

The third element of a big idea is the signature solution. This is the unique way you help your customers solve their big problem and achieve the big goal.

Let's say obesity is the big problem you want to solve and your big goal is to help people lose 100 pounds in six weeks (and keep those pounds off forever). The next step in the new factory thinking process is to determine the best way for people to achieve this objective. After doing research and perhaps a series of experiments, you conclude that hopping on one leg for 60 minutes each day will do the trick. You call this approach *The Hopping Method*. You then promote this method in the marketplace by writing educational blogs and producing videos about this innovative approach.

Let's imagine you help people with their finances. The big problem is that most people in retirement run out of money before they die and have to rely on family or the state to cover the shortfall. The big goal is to help people have three times more income during retirement than they were expecting. Your signature solution is a unique investing method based on the hoarding strategies of the Western Scrub Jay, a bird species found in Western North America. You developed this theory by combining your interest in investing with your passion for bird watching. You call this special technique *The Scrub Jay Portfolio System*.

Let's speculate you want to help manufacturers increase their operating efficiencies. The big problem is that most manufacturers waste significant energy and human resources due to inefficient supply chain processes. Your big goal is to help manufacturers increase their throughput capacity by 500 percent within three years. Based on your experience and experimentation over two decades, you develop a close-looped feedback reporting system that continuously improves supply chain efficiencies. You call this approach *The Entropic Spiral.*

Notice that each of these signature solutions is a theory or concept, not a specific product or service. This gives your business another immutable anchor that won't be swept away by unpredictable change in the future. Even more compelling is that the signature solution belongs to you and only you. It's your theory. It's your approach. As a new factory thinker, you build your brand around something that none of your competitors can emulate. You understand that it's impossible for one of your competitors to say they also use *The Scrub Jay Portfolio System* or *The Entropic Spiral* because only you know how it really works.

By creating and packaging a signature solution, you become a gourmet chef in a marketplace of hot dog vendors. You put together a unique meal that is not only more interesting, but it also works better. This is, of course, another key feature of the signature solution. It isn't smoke and mirrors and a bunch of marketing hokum, it's actually works.

Your signature solution doesn't come out of thin air. It comes by combining your education, experience, and interests with the intention to solve a big problem and achieve a big goal. That's why new factory thinking is more empowering than its predecessor. It empowers you to combine previously disparate parts of yourself into a coherent whole that provides value in the world—a lot of value.

Once you have identified your signature solution, you need to test it. You need to find ten or more subjects who will participate in a beta test. Typically you don't charge them anything because they are doing you a favor. Based on the results of each test, you incrementally refine all aspects of your theory, including the process, the tools used, and the forms of communication. For example, you might discover that no one can get their head around *The Entropic Spiral*, and change its name to *The Intrinsic Feedback Formula*.

It's important to remember that your signature solution is not about what you do; it's about what you know. Based on your years of experience, you've learned what works and what doesn't. You know what your customers do wrong, and what will help them achieve better results. What we're doing at this stage is excavating this knowledge and putting it front and center.

Nick Bloor, one of my clients in Australia, developed a method for managing large-scale property management projects. He called it *Integrated Vegetation Management* or *IVM*. His company had used this method internally for more than a decade until they turned it into intellectually property. They now sell the IVM system to cities and large corporate clients, and sub-contract out the property management to other companies, including their former competitors.

"My old factory was my *doing* business," Nick told me one day. "My new factory is my *thinking* business."

Nick's comment hit the nail on the head. Old factory thinkers believe the only way to make money is to *do* something for a customer. New factory thinkers know it's better and more lucrative to get paid for what you know, not what you do. That's why it's a good idea to do a complete inventory of your knowledge base. You will undercover priceless ideas, wisdom, and creative solutions that have been gathering dust in the recesses of your mind.

To determine your signature solution, start with a blank slate. Don't think about your existing products/services or your industry. Contemplate your customer's situation. What do they need to do differently in order to solve the big problem and achieve the big goal? Imagine that anything is possible and there are no restrictions on resources.

Make your signature solution the centerpiece of your marketing. Educate your prospects about the problem—i.e. 32% of people are unnecessarily obese. Tell them the big goal—to help people lose 100 pounds in 6 weeks. Explain the signature solution—hop on one leg for an hour a day. Then coach them through a step-by-step process designed to achieve that result—i.e. *The Hopping Method*.

To reiterate, the signature solution is not a product or service in itself; it's a theory or concept. It acts as the axel of your value hub, which could contain hundreds, even thousands, of products or services. That's the beauty of it. Rather than restrict what you can offer your customers, the signature solution infinitely expands your potential storehouse of products and services. We'll cover this concept more in step five: the one-stop store.

Finding the exact signature solution might take time. Don't become too attached to the first thing that comes to mind. Test and refine your signature solution. Start off with something general and move to something more specific. When I started my business in the late 1980s, I discovered that most entrepreneurs did not have a marketing plan. I observed that most business owners, if they did any marketing at all, focused on marketing tools (like advertising or websites), rather than strategy. I called this *The Marketing Tools Trap*. My signature solution was to help them develop a marketing plan. That worked well, but it was a pretty generic solution and made me vulnerable to competition. I recognized that anyone could say they help business owners create a marketing plan.

To be more specific, I zeroed in more and asked myself: what is the key component of a marketing plan? I concluded it was a big idea; something one-of-a-kind that would help my clients stand out from their competition. Without a big idea, I knew, the marketing plan probably wouldn't work. So I fine-tuned my approach. The big problem became *The Penguin Problem* (it's hard to stand out from the other *penguins* in your industry). The signature solution was to devise and package a big idea—*The BIG Idea Adventure*.

My new signature solution worked much better. By being more specific, it was easier for my prospects to get their head around what I was proposing. Secondly, it had a much higher barrier to entry. Many people can create a marketing plan, but only a handful of people can come up with a big idea. In fact, I've never had anyone try to compete with me in the big idea space, which essentially means I have no competition.

So don't worry if your signature solution is relatively simple at first. It doesn't have to be fancy. The answer to your customers' problems might be very straightforward. They just need someone to point out the big problem and help them solve it. Remember, your old factory competitors aren't thinking like you are. They concentrate on pushing their products and services. The only problem in their minds is that the customer isn't buying enough of their product. That's why a company like Uber trumped the taxi companies. The taxi companies were focused on selling cab rides. They weren't thinking about how to use new technology to add value to the taxi experience.

Two final points. One, remember that your big goal is merely an intention, not a promise. You can't guarantee that everyone you work with will always achieve the big goal. But you have the intention to try and make it happen by continually honing your signature solution.

Second, the best signature solutions are a combination of skills, talents and resources that have never been integrated before. In my case, I combined my experiences as a waiter (how to sell a lobster), my education in journalism school (words and stories), and my passion for innovation (big ideas). That's why this process is so powerful. It enables you to integrate previously separate parts of yourself into a complete whole that provides tremendous value in the marketplace. It empowers you to get paid handsomely for skills and abilities that were previously dormant, fragmented or under-utilized.

COMMUNICATING YOUR BIG IDEA

Significant value can be delivered with words. By using the right words to communicate complex ideas in a simple manner, you help your customers quickly recognize previously undiagnosed problems and start working on big goals they've never tried to pursue before. But you have to communicate these concepts effectively. You only have a few seconds to get your message across. If you use the right words, you will steer them away from the wrong path and onto a better path. Years later they'll look back and realize that the moment you explained your big idea—and they got it—was a key turning point in their life or their business.

So start honing the communication of your big idea. Tell people about the big goal and the big problem. Tell them about the signature solution. Don't keep it a secret. Tell everyone. This testing will quickly hone your ideas and your message. You'll discover what ideas are compelling and which ones fall flat. You'll learn what words resonate in the marketplace and what words do not. In no time, you will have a polished story for your big idea.

A few additional tips. Don't sound like a salesperson. Be enthusiastic, but don't push your big idea. Be matter of fact about it. Additionally, don't get discouraged if some people disparage your idea. That's to be expected. Many people are wired for negativity. They jump on people who think big. But these people don't matter. Look for positive people who appreciate and applaud what you're trying to do.

Remember, most people are still wired for old factory thinking. They haven't read this book—yet. As a leader, be prepared for resistance and doubt. That's part of the challenge but also the opportunity. By taking a leadership position, you take the hard road, but it's the road that leads to opportunity.

Action Plan

1. Once again, think about your customers. What is the one thing they need to do differently in order to solve the big problem and achieve the big goal? What is the activity, strategy, or thought-process that will make a difference?

2. Consider: What different skills, talents, and resources can you combine to help your customers achieve the big goal? Start with a blank slate: Allow yourself to consider previously unimaginable solutions. Invite your team, associates, customers, and even your competitors to help you determine the signature solution.

3. Give the signature solution a name like *The Hopping Method* or *The Entropic Spiral.*

4. Test your big idea (big goal, big problem and signature solution) by telling 10 people about it.

CHAPTER 10

STEP 3: FREE VALUE

In the new factory era, there is a free lunch. You can get free telephone service, free online access, free college courses, and free consultations. Free everything.

Today's smart marketers know that the best way to attract lots of prospects is to give them something for free. It's like giving out a free piece of chocolate. You can spend a small fortune advertising your box of chocolate or you can give out free samples. In a marketplace where prospects distain salespeople and use voice mail and spam filters to block them out, giving away free value is the best solution.

Old factory thinkers don't give any value until the customer makes a purchase. They make a sales pitch. They tell customers about their product's features and benefits. They quote a price. And if the customer forks over the money, the old factory thinker provides the promised value.

New factory thinkers, on the other hand, provide value *during* the sales process. They give their prospects something for free—such as knowledge, tools or ideas. They realize that the free value strategy is much easier, less expensive, and more effective than the old factory sales approach.

A few years back, my wife signed up for Skype. She was amazed that she could call anywhere in the world—for free. "This is great," she said, "but how does Skype make any money when they give away their product for free?" I explained that free internet telephone service is not Skype's real business, it's their marketing strategy, what has come to be known as the "fremium" model. Using this model, you give away something for free in order to sign up a certain percentage of the people to a premium program.

You've probably experienced the freemium approach yourself, especially online. In my case, I've signed up for several for-pay premium programs after sampling a free offering. I'm a premium user on Skype, LinkedIn, Google, and numerous other cloud-based business services.

Bear in mind that the free value strategy is not just for online businesses. It can be extended to any kind of business, online or offline. Instead of trying to sell on features, benefits, or price, you simply give away something of value in order to attract more prospects.

Understanding and using this principle helped me grow my business exponentially. In the past, I told prospects I would help them create and package a big idea if they hired me. But this traditional sales approach didn't work very well. My prospects couldn't visualize a big idea or what it would do for them. So I decided to give away big ideas instead. Now, I offer prospects a free big idea conversation. In the session I help them identify their big idea and craft a new elevator speech for them. Using this free value approach, I close more sales faster because my prospects don't just hear about my box of chocolate, they get to taste the chocolate for free.

Free value can take many forms: such as ideas, knowledge, online services, or apps. You can give away your time, your attention or your assistance. Ideally, the free value should be related to what you sell. If you sell travel services, there's no point is giving prospects a free oil change.

Don't attach any strings to your free value. For example, a 10 percent discount is not free value. A sales presentation is not free value. Telling your prospects about testimonials is not free value. It needs to be something truly useful that is not tied to a purchase.

Free value gives you more leverage in your relationship with prospects. To get the free value, your prospects need to give you a few things in return. At a minimum, they need to give you their name and email address, and grant you permission to communicate with them on a regular basis (see Seth Goden's book *Permission Marketing*). They may also need to give you their time and attention so you can get to know them better.

Prospects who seek out your fee value become *subscribers*. This designation is appropriate because they are people who subscribe to your big idea. They like it and they get it. They might not be able to join your premium program yet, but they are supporters of what you are doing.

It's important not to pull a bait-and-switch on your subscribers. When you send them information or invite them to events like a webinar, don't make a sales pitch. Your emails and events should be useful, educational, and even entertaining. Otherwise, a lot of your prospects will unsubscribe.

New factory thinkers understand that providing free value during the sales process is the best way to attract prospects in the 21st Century marketplace. They realize many commodity products and services offered by old factories can become the free value of new factories. Back in the 1980s, I worked on the marketing for a national mobile telephone company (called a cellular telephone company in those days). At that time, cellphones cost $1,800 and had to be hard-wired into your car. But I could see what was going to happen. I told people that one day cellular companies would give away the phones for free in order to sign customers to service contracts. No one believed me. The thought of giving away an $1,800 product was absurd. But now, service providers give away mobile phones in exchange for a two- or three-year contract. So watch out. A new factory might start giving away your product or service in order to attract more members. That's why it's important to create value that transcends your old factory competitors so it doesn't matter if your product or service becomes free value fodder.

Of course, you can take the lead on this and give away your product or service for free in order to sell customers a higher-margin new factory program. You could also give away another company's products for free. One of my clients who sells college education financing plans created something called *The New Mother Registry*. Expectant mothers register on the website and receive dozens of free samples, like diapers and baby food. They also get a free consultation with a college-funding expert. This is an excellent free value strategy for my client because he doesn't have to provide the free products. Other companies do. And every year, more than 50,000 mothers register for the program, which results in more than 10,000 college funding sales for the company.

To adopt this aspect of new factory thinking, you have to overcome your entrenched sales mindset. You have to stop talking about your products and services. Stop trying to prove that your products are better than your competitors. Stop pitching. Just give away something for free. You will save a lot of time, money, and energy, and attract a lot more prospects. Of course, some of these prospects will be freeloaders. But that's okay. That comes with the territory. But you will also meet more ideal customers who are ready to buy after they have sampled the free value. This will result in more members and more sales.

Action Plan

1. Brainstorm ideas for your free value. What could you offer for free that would be appealing to your prospects?

2. Experiment on a few prospects. Offer them the free value and see if they're interested in it. Find the right balance between giving too little and giving too much. (You only need to offer enough to attract the prospect. If one piece of chocolate will do it, there is no point in giving them two pieces.)

3. Develop a two-tiered free value system. Give every prospect one piece of chocolate. Then qualify them to see which ones are potential members. Offer these ideal prospects additional chocolate. This two-tiered approach will help you further engage the ideal prospects in order to turn them into members (see next chapter).

CHAPTER 11

STEP 4: MEMBERSHIP PROGRAM

Recently I gave a presentation about the new factory to an association of entrepreneurs. The event was held at the Microsoft store at a local mall. Interestingly, the Apple store was next door. With an hour to kill before my presentation I took a look around the two stores. For the most part, I couldn't see much difference between the two. Both Apple and Microsoft have great products. They have friendly and knowledgeable staff. And they are both innovative. But there's one huge difference. When I visited the Microsoft store, I saw *customers*. When I went into the Apple store, I saw *members*. In my opinion that's the reason why Apple continues to grow while Microsoft flounders. Microsoft is an old factory that focuses first on its products while Apple is a new factory that focuses first on getting members.

This is a tricky concept to get, especially if you are still wired for old factory thinking. After all, it's just two different words: customer and member. Why would they create such a different outcome? It's all about consciousness. When you purchase a product from an old factory, you do so because you like its features and price. You could even be a fanatic about the product. You think it's the best product in the world. But your loyalty only runs so deep. If another company releases a superior product at a better price, you would be tempted to switch allegiances.

However, when you're a member of a new factory, you have a

much different relationship with the company. Being a member is not just about owning a product or using a service, it's about who you are as a person. Being a member is part of your self-image, an integral part of your lifestyle. Even if a competitor comes out with a better product, you are unlikely to switch because then you would have to change your personal self-image.

I consider myself to be an Apple person. I've been using Apple computers and most of their other products since the early 1980s. I live and breathe inside the Apple eco-system. When it comes to my relationship with Apple, I have *membership consciousness*. My relationship with the company is integral to who I am. I feel part of a larger community, all of us united by our membership with Apple.

I have membership consciousness with several other companies including American Express, Costco, and Amazon. With Amex, I enjoy the fact that my card gives me free exclusive access to airport lounges around the world. With Costco, I like saving money by buying in bulk. And with Amazon, I have become habituated to always check their store before I buy anything. Most of the time I end up buying the product from Amazon because I've set up a fast and reliable delivery system that saves me a lot of time and money. I am also a subscriber to Amazon Prime, which for one annual fee, gives me unlimited no-additional-charge shipping.

New factories create membership programs because they want to build a wall around their customers as a bulwark against increased competition. They don't want their customers stolen away. They want to steal customers. That's what Amazon has done to Staples. Many Amazon customers, who began by buying books from the company, now buy their office supplies from them as well. This means that Staples has been undermined, not by another office supply company, but by a book company. It's unlikely that Staples, lost in old factory thinking, saw that coming.

Creating membership consciousness is critical in the new factory marketplace because the cost of sales is skyrocketing. As I explained earlier, it's harder than ever to capture a high-quality customer. As such, it's unwise to only sell one thing to a hard-won customer. Once you have their trust, you want to sell them as much as you can for as long as you can. That's why new factories like Apple, Google and Amazon offer so many products and services in their one-stop store (see next chapter).

It's easy to start a membership program. Begin by deciding what members get that regular customers don't get. This can be exclusive access, additional features, enhanced technology, or invitations to member-only events. My Amex card not only gives me access to the airport lounges, it also gives me first crack at concert tickets. My premium membership on LinkedIn gives me enhanced features like expanded profiling capabilities. As a member at my local art gallery, I am invited to special parties and previews of art exhibits.

What you offer your members is only limited by your imagination. Anything they would find valuable, or would make them feel special, might be a good idea. One of my members, Chris Hotze, created an innovative membership benefit that he initially thought wouldn't work. For his old factory, Chris sold real estate investments in the Houston area. For his new factory, he created *The Winning Line-up Program*. Once members have invested their money in one of Chris's projects, they also receive a package of additional benefits including exclusive access to a wine locker at one of

Houston's most expensive restaurants.

"At first, I thought the wine locker idea was nonsense," Chris said. "But then I found it captured the imagination of my prospects. In fact, I recently signed up three members and all they could talk about was the wine locker. This sort of approach has completely changed how I see my business and what constitutes value in the mind of the customer."

The key is to have two levels: customer and member. Prospects need to decide which one they want. Do they want to do a simple transaction and become a customer, or do they want to take the premium package and become a member? Of course, if they become a member, they have to pay more and be more involved in the process. It's also important that they buy into the big idea. They have to be willing participants in achieving the big goal, solving the big problem, and doing the signature activity.

Creating a membership program solves a lot of the problems that afflict old factories. One, it helps you communicate the reason why prospects should choose your company over a competitor. Two, it demonstrates all of the added value you deliver. Three, if they choose the program, they are willing to pay a premium price. And four, it builds a wall around your customers so they won't switch as readily to your competitors.

There are two kinds of membership programs, integrated and non-integrated. In an integrated program, your members have a relationship with each other. Facebook and LinkedIn have integrated programs. This is the best kind of program because its binds your members even more tightly to your company. If they stop being a member or switch to a competitor, integrated member not only have to leave you, they have to leave the other members. Non-integrated memberships are not as good in this regard, but in some cases, new factories prefer to keep members separated from each other. This is the case with Apple and Amazon.

Membership consciousness is reinforced in several ways. One, the very act of choosing the membership level over the basic customer level gives your customers a sense of empowerment. They choose to be a member. It isn't forced on them. Secondly, it's important to keep reminding them that they are members. Send them emails about new membership features. Give them a membership card. Third, reward active members with points, recognition or bonus features.

Start by looking at your list of existing customers. Separate them into two categories, ideal and not-ideal. Make the ideal customers honorary members. Inform them that they don't need to pay anything extra to be a member. You just want to acknowledge that they are special. This strategy helps you build a wall around your best existing customers. It also gives you a group of potential guinea pigs to test out the features of your membership program.

Make it your primary marketing objective to add more members. You can still do business with customers who come along, but getting a member is worth 20 customers. It's the difference between selling a hot dog or selling a gourmet meal. Just imagine if you had 100 or even 10,000 members who are just like your existing ideal customers. What would your business look like then?

Delineate what members get that non-members don't get. Think big. Think up as many potential features that could be included in the membership program. Note that you don't need to offer all of these things at first. In fact, it's better if you don't. That way, you can introduce more features in the future. Ideally, look beyond your company and your industry to find resources to include in the program. Include other experts, products, and services that have never been offered in your industry before.

Once you have your main program outlined, consider having three levels: such as bronze, silver and gold. What would members get at each level? How much would you charge for each level? Would bronze members need to work their way up to silver and gold?

Pricing can be a challenge for some budding new factory thinkers. They're held back by the notion that everyone is looking for the cheapest price. They're afraid to charge a lot because they think they will scare away customers. But that's not true. That's why we keep the basic customer level. Customers can still buy your competitively-priced products and services. You haven't raised your prices. You're simply giving them higher-level options that provide more value at a higher price. The pleasant surprise comes when prospects choose the membership program confirming the marketing principle: If you charge more, some of your customers will want it more. The only danger is not offering a higher-priced membership program because if you don't someone else will.

When you meet prospects, preferably by giving them free value, you will be in position to size them up. Are they a potential customer or a potential member? As time goes by, you'll get better at making this distinction. You won't spend as much time on low-opportunity customers, which will enable you to devote more time and attention to high-opportunity members.

Tell prospects your advanced program is not for everyone. Make it clear that you don't take everyone in your program. It's exclusive and hard to get into. This will make them want it even more and make them feel extra special when they get in.

Turning your customers into members also generates more high-quality referrals. To reinforce their experience, members like to recruit their friends and family to become members too. Bringing others into the fold validates their own decision of becoming a member, and also enhances the value of their experience.

It's important that the membership program is not free. Making it free undermines the perceived value of the program and cuts into your profits. In some cases, you can waive the fee if you are compensated in another way, such as by commissions on the sale of products. Either way, the membership program needs to have a stated value, such as $500, 10,000 or a million dollars.

Your membership program also needs a step-by-step process. You need to walk your members through this process in a methodical manner. Having a process gives the program structure and a sense of momentum. Members feel they are constantly moving away from the big problem and towards the big goal. Ideally, use a tool such as a scorecard or reward points to chart this progress. Give members credits or prizes to acknowledge the achievement of milestones. Make it fun and interactive.

Bear in mind that not everyone will want to be a member of your program. Some people won't get the big idea or they won't be willing to pay the membership fee. That's okay. They can still be a customer. But as time goes by, you'll find a large contingent of ideal people and your membership will grow; slowly at first and then with faster acceleration. In my case, it took me 12 months to sign up my first 50 members, and then in one month I signed up 30 members.

Continually improve your program. Start with version one: a simple package of membership benefits. When appropriate, add more features to version two. For each version, increase the price if you want. Each time you come out with a new version, inform your members and subscribers. In my case, we are now on version eight of our membership program and working on version nine.

Keep track of how many members have joined your program, and tell everyone the current number. Use a cumulative numbering system so the number never goes down. In other words, keep track of how many members you have ever had, not how many you have at any time.

When you reach a critical mass of members, the program will take on a life of its own. Members will bring in new members. People will start talking about your program and wonder aloud whether they should join. The world will be divided into two groups: members of your program and people who aren't members.

Action Plan

1. Make a list of all the potential things you could provide your members. Add value components from other companies and from outside your industry.

2. Determine what your members get that non-members don't get for version one of your program.

3. Make a list of your existing ideal customers. Make them honorary members. Try out the program features on them. Refine your program based on this experience.

4. Tell prospects they have two choices: to become a customer or become a member. If they're interested in being a member, make them go through a process to qualify.

5. Begin by charging a modest sum for the first few members and then gradually raise the fee until you meet or exceed your target price.

6. Continually improve your program by changing and adding new features.

CHAPTER 12

STEP 5: ONE-STOP STORE

The ultimate payoff for a new factory is the one-stop store. Instead of selling customers one or two things, the new factory sells its members a lot of things. Even better, most of the products and services sold in the one-stop store are created and delivered by other companies. This generates low-risk passive income for the new factory and keeps its members from venturing outside its value hub.

In a marketplace with hard-to-engage prospects and a high cost of sales, a one-stop store enables a new factory to maximize the lifetime value of its members. By selling a lot of products and services to each customer, the new factory recoups and exceeds the upfront costs of acquiring that customer.

This is a not a new idea. My great-great-grandfather Timothy Eaton built a department store empire in Canada based on a similar concept. Instead of going to different vendors, customers could shop at one store—Eatons—and get everything they needed. Customers enjoyed the convenience and also felt reassured by the company's refund policy. Once they came to trust Eatons they didn't feel the need to shop anywhere else.

More than a century later, and in a much different kind of marketplace, the principles of the one-stop store still apply. Once you get used to buying from a company, and come to trust them, you are open to buying other things from that company. That's why Apple had success when it moved into the music business. Its established customers were ready, willing and able to buy music from them. The same applies to Amazon as it expands beyond its initial offering—books—into thousands of other products.

Creating a one-stop store is not only good idea, it's an imperative. If you don't do it, a new factory competitor will do it first. One of the members of my program Rick Caouette created a new factory called *The Right Now Program*. Rick's old factory provided air filters to major airlines. His new factory features a one-stop online store where airlines can source hard-to-find aircraft parts from hundreds of suppliers. Rick makes money from the purchase of every part sold through his store. His website is now the first place his members look when they need a part, any part.

The point is this: if Rick hadn't created his one-stop store, another player in his industry, or from outside his industry, would have created it. If that had happened, Rick's company would have been merely a supplier in someone else's one-stop store. Instead of earning passive income from hundreds of transactions, he would have been paying tribute to another new factory.

Taking initiative in this way is surprisingly easy. You don't need to invent new products and services; you simply need to aggregate them for your members. The world is awash in resources, they just need to be compiled and packaged in a way that makes it easy for your members to access and purchase them.

While the idea is simple in concept, many companies struggle with the idea of a one-stop store because of their old factory thinking. The self-image they have of their company is based on their traditional products and services. They can't imagine selling products from other companies, or from outside their industry. They certainly can't conceive of selling their competitors' products. It just doesn't fit into their worldview.

A few months back, I spoke at a financial services conference in Texas. Following my presentation about the new factory, they had a panel of experts from the big banks who discussed the future of the financial services industry. A number of the pundits expressed concern that Apple, Google, or Amazon might make a foray into their industry. At one point I stood up and said: "You better start worrying because it's inevitable. It will be so easy for those companies to add financial services to their one-stop store."

Having lots of members is what gives you leverage over suppliers to your one-stop store. Music, movie and app companies are willing to give Apple a 30% commission on every sale because Apple has what they don't have—members.

Once sales start to flow through your one-stop store, your single-minded focus on your traditional products will wane. When you make low-risk passive income, high-risk active income becomes less appealing. Last week, I made a sale through my one-stop store. I had referred a member to a commercial designer. She sold them $13,0000 worth of services and sent me a check for $1,300. The total amount of time I spent on the transaction was about five minutes. That worked out to $26,000 per hour!

With the value hub model in mind, new factory thinkers see their business as a central station where members and suppliers meet. They don't worry what products and services are sold—they simply bring buyers and sellers together. This is the model used by thousands of emerging new factories like Uber and Airbnb. These are the purest new factories because they never had an old factory in the first place.

Bear in mind that you don't need to have millions of offerings in your one-stop store. You might have ten or 50, depending on what your members need. You simply explore what your members already buy, and would buy, and decide if it makes sense to put the products and services in your store. The value you provide is two-fold. One, you assess the quality and reliability of each supplier so your members don't have to. Second, by aggregating these previously disparate resources into one place, you save your members time, money and effort.

To facilitate the transactions in your one-stop store, you have two options. The risker option is to collect the money and then pay the supplier. This is risky because the purchaser will hold you primarily responsible for the transaction. If something goes wrong, they will contact you and request a refund. You will then need to extract a refund from the supplier. Better to have the member and supplier do the primary transaction and then get the supplier to forward you the commission. If the deal goes sideways you aren't involved, and if the supplier doesn't pay the commission, you are not out-of-pocket. This is how I run my one-stop store and it works beautifully. I simply bring buyer and seller together and collect my commission.

Remember that you hold all of the cards in your relationship with the supplier. Because you have lots of members, suppliers want to get access to them. As such, you can dictate the terms of the arrangement. You can ask for 10, 20 or 30% on each transaction. No matter how onerous the terms, they will likely go along because they know you can always find another supplier for their commodity product. But even then, they probably won't mind because you are doing all the marketing for them. They just have to deliver the product. So it's a good deal for them no matter what. That's why the one-stop store is a win-win situation for everyone involved. You make high-margin passive income. The supplier gets customers they wouldn't get otherwise. And the customer gets the convenience and potential efficiencies of buying lots of things in one place.

Creating a one-stop store significantly increases the value your members receive from you. It enables you to seamlessly incorporate other capabilities that were previously beyond the scope of your old factory. One of the members of my program runs a security guard company in Columbia. It was a low-margin, high-volume business that had become a commodity. He had many competitors offering basically the same services, so he created a big idea called *The Convergent Security Program* to help his members develop an integrated company-wide security plan that addresses key issues of employee theft, terrorism and cyber-crime. He was initially wary of offering these services because he believed that they were beyond his company's expertise. To help him get his one-stop store off the ground I introduced him to another one of my members, a leading expert in cyber-crime. Now he receives thousands of dollars a year from the work done by the cyber-crime company.

Building a one-stop store also helps you escape from the self-defeating competitive stance of old factory thinkers. In many cases, new factory thinkers add the products and services of their competitors to their one-stop store. Why not? There is no better feeling that making money selling your competitors' products, especially when you make a better profit on the transaction than they do. If you can get your mind around this notion, you will be a undeniable new factory thinker.

There's an important consideration to keep in mind when implementing this strategy. Don't go out and start amassing suppliers willy-nilly. You might waste your time setting up suppliers for products and services that your members don't want. Instead, speak to your customers. Find out what they want. When a need becomes apparent, source a supplier and add them to your store. Grow your store organically based on the needs of your members.

It's likely that you already have the makings of a one-stop store. You certainly have your own products and services, and you may already refer customers to other suppliers. Going forward, develop more formal arrangements with these suppliers regarding remuneration for referrals.

Also note that you don't necessarily need a website to host your one-stop store. It is necessary if you sell hard goods like aircraft parts, but your business might be different. For example, if you're a financial advisor, you might refer members to suppliers by giving them a telephone number or through a personal introduction. No website is needed. That's another reminder that a new factory does not need to be technologically driven. You can run a new factory with a telephone, a pen, and pad of paper. The new factory model is universally applicable and is not dependent on transitory technologies.

Action Plan

1. Make a list of your company's products and services. Create another list of other products and services that your customers buy from other companies and other industries.

2. Tell your members that they can have access to these additional products and services.

3. Source new suppliers when the need arises. Vet them carefully to make sure they do a high-quality job.

4. Make formal arrangements for remuneration from these suppliers. (Note: In some cases, you might not want to receive a commission for referrals to suppliers. You may simply want to provide the one-stop store as a member benefit.)

SECTION THREE

NEW FACTORY VALUE CREATION

CHAPTER 13

LESS RESOURCES

In the old factory era, the best way to make money was to get your customers to consume more resources; cars, oil, electricity, appliances, clothing, food, pet rocks, and a million other things. The more your customers consumed, the more money you made. In the new factory era, the way to make money is to help your customers achieve better results using *less* resources. (Resources in this context means time, effort, energy, raw materials, and money).

Consider the sharing economy. Close to my home is a tool library. For a $50 a year membership, you can borrow more than 3,000 tools such as hammers, saws, and ladders. If you want to make three holes in your living room, you don't need to pay $85 for a drill from the hardware store. You can borrow the drill from the library for no charge.

Consider smart thermostats. They learn your lifestyle habits and optimize your energy consumption so you can stay comfortable— warm in the winter, cool in the summer—while spending less money. Smart thermostats are part of more integrated home automation systems that enable you to control lighting, security systems and appliances, once again helping you save time and energy.

Consider WAZE. Unlike other navigation systems that simply plot your route and provide basic traffic reports, WAZE is a free collaborative navigation system that taps into the shared knowledge of its members. WAZE monitors traffic conditions by collecting information from each member currently on the road. If another WAZE member is stuck in traffic, the system advises you to take another route. As networks like WAZE expand, the amount of useful information also grows, thereby helping members save even more time and energy by directing them to even more efficient routes.

The sharing economy, smart systems, and collaborative networks are just three of the tools that will drive the new factory marketplace in the coming decades. As the economy makes its full transition to the new factory era, consumers will be empowered to save increasingly more time, money and effort using less resources in all areas of their life. A great example of this transformation is the music industry. In the past, if you wanted to purchase a song, you had to consume a lot of resources. You got in your car and drove to a store in order to buy a vinyl record. Then you drove home and put the record on a turntable. After listening to the song a few times, you stored the record on a shelf. It became part of your collection. That was a lot of resources needed to listen to one song. The amount of resources was even larger if we add in what was needed to make the car, produce the record, deliver it to the store, operate the store, and manufacture the turntable. When you take in the whole picture, the resources-per-song goes through the roof.

In the new factory marketplace, you can listen to a song using much fewer resources. You can go online and choose a song or album from a streaming service like Apple Music that costs $10 a month for an unlimited subscription. There are 30 million songs to choose from. You don't have to leave your house and it takes a few seconds. The resources-per-song is minuscule.

Granted, many people lost their job when the old factory music industry went kaput. These victims of change included the people who manufactured the vinyl record, the driver who delivered the record to the store, the people who worked in the store, and the people who built the store and turntable. Recording artists also complain that they don't make as much money per song. But the consumer is thrilled because they get a better result for less time, money and effort.

The incentive to save money by using less resources is one of the key factors driving the emergence of the new factory marketplace. As computers become faster and smarter and more people and things connect on the Internet, it becomes possible to get more for less in every aspect of our lives. As a result, more and more things will become better and also less resource intensive. They will also be less expensive. In his book *The Zero Marginal Cost Society*, Jeremy Rifkin contends that most traditional (old factory) products and services will become virtually free:

As more goods and services becoming nearly free, fewer purchases are being made in the marketplace, reducing GDP. Even those items still being purchased are becoming fewer in number as more people redistribute and recycle previously purchased goods in the sharable economy. A growing legion of consumers are also opting for access over ownership of goods, preferring to pay only for the limited time they use a car, bicycle, toy, tool or other item.

As old factory products and services face downward price pressure towards zero profit margin, the question remains: How can companies survive in this environment? Why would companies continue to provide their products for free? Why would they and how could they? Of course, you know the answer. New factories will give away traditional products and services for free to entice prospects into their membership programs.

To become a new factory thinker, you need to abandon your resource-intensive mindset. Create new kinds of value by helping your customers get better results with less resources. Ask: How can we help them save time? How can we help them save energy and effort? How can we help them use less raw materials?

Many old factory thinkers do not like this principle. They think it's left-leaning environmental hogwash. They think they will make less money if their customers use less resources. That's why banks want their customers to use their credit cards as much as possible. Electrical utilities want their customers to use more energy. And the food service industry wants their customers to eat more fast food. But that's where the problem lies. The intentions and incentives of old factories are at cross-purposes to the best interests of their customers. Of course they deny it, but isn't it true? Do banks want their customers to use their credit cards less? Of course not. Do utilities want their customers to cut down on electricity use? Not a chance. Does the fast food industry advocate that the populace eat less hamburgers and french fries? Don't be absurd. Old factories want their customers to consume more because that's how they make money.

Forget the moral and ethical ramifications of this issue. I'm not asking you to become a tree-hugging saint and tell your customers to use less of your product. I want you to make more money. I'm just saying that the consume-more approach isn't good business anymore.

Your customers now have alternatives. Everyday, new factories are emerging to give them novel ways to get better results for less money, less time, and less effort. So the choice is yours: You can either be one of these new factories or you can let a competitor do it.

Old factories are dying because their goals are not the same as their customers' goals. They strive to become more profitable by using less resources in their operations (less people, overhead, and input costs), while encouraging their customers to consume more resources. But new factories are eclipsing old factories because they have the same goals as their customers. While they try to use less resources themselves, new factories also try to help their customers use less resources. In other words, new factories are on the same team as their customers. Old factories aren't.

The underlying assumption of the old factory culture was that *more consumption equals more happiness.* Keeping the assembly lines moving meant economic growth and jobs. Consuming more was the way to make your contribution to society. In the new factory marketplace, a new equation for success is ascending: *Achieve more well-being using less resources.* Incentives and capabilities are now in place for a new worldview based on these new aspirations: Use less energy. Waste less time. Get things done easier. Spend less money on commodities. Be healthier. Be more content. Feel more secure. Feel more fulfilled. Feel more connected.

Unfortunately, this opportunity is lost on many old factory thinkers. Recently, I met a young entrepreneur in the railroad industry. His company does maintenance on railcars. His business model is simple: get paid by the hour for doing maintenance on railcars. I suggested that he build a new factory to make money in a different way. Instead of charging by the hour, he would charge based on results. He told me that an independent research study determined that a railroad company that did proactive maintenance on all its railcars would save millions due to less downtime and accidents. I asked him how much his typical customer might save. He said they could easily save $50 million a year. I said: "If you could cut their costs by $50 million, wouldn't they be willing to give you $10 million for that result?" Instead of getting paid for his services by the hour, which is seen as an expenditure by the customer, he could get paid by results, and be seen as cost-saver. But he couldn't see the opportunity. His old factory mind was stuck on: We make money maintaining railcars and get paid by the hour. In fact, he became rather irritated by my suggestion, as if I was insulting his old factory. Too bad. I was just trying to figure out how he could make $10 million by helping his customer save $50 million.

In the new factory marketplace, you are not going to make money by getting your customers to consume more. You are going to make money by helping your customers consume less. When you come to grips with this principle, you'll have a firm foundation as a new factory thinker.

CHAPTER 14

UNDER-UTILIZED RESOURCES

I'm guessing you probably own a couch. How often do you sit on it? Let's estimate it's 10% of the time, tops. The rest of the time, it just waits for you to sit down and watch a movie. But what if you could turn that other 90% of unused couch time into something of value, for both yourself and others? That's what a new factory called CouchSurfing does. It's a platform that enables its members to share their couches with travellers. While the couch-owner doesn't make any money—the couches are offered for free—both the coucher and couchee get social value from the exchange. Most participants report that the coach surfing concept helps them meet new people from different countries and cultures. In August 2014, the company reported it had more than 10 million people in its community.

The CouchSurfing story illustrates another way that new factory thinkers provide value: by enabling their members to make the best use of under-utilized resources. In this regard, they provide value in two ways: they give their members access to the dormant resources of others and also enable them to sell or share their own idle resources.

Look around. The new factory marketplace is exploding with this kind of value creation. Uber helps its drivers turn their personal vehicles into a moneymaker, much to the chagrin of traditional taxi drivers. Airbnb allows its members to save money on hotels by accessing the homes of its resources partners. Shared Earth is an organization that brings together urban farmers with homeowners who have vacant land that can be turned into a vegetable garden. Liquid Space is an online platform that enables its members to rent out by the hour the unused meeting rooms in their office. I'm an avid user of *HomeForExchange.com*. Over the past few years, my wife and I have exchanged our home and cottage with several other members. We recently did an exchange in Germany. A German family stayed in our house and we stayed in theirs. Both parties had a great holiday and it didn't cost a penny for the accommodations.

These new factories are attracting millions of members and millions of suppliers because their value proposition is a win-win for everyone. Typically, one party saves money and the other party makes money on something that had previously been an expense, rather than a profit center.

The economic incentives inherent in this new factory concept will have a profound impact on our economy and society. As I will discuss more in an upcoming chapter, access will soon trump ownership as the primary way to use resources. Owning a car that sits idle most of the time—while incurring costs 100% of the time—will one day seem ludicrous. Rather, people who own a car will think nothing of renting it out on an hourly basis, and people who don't own a car will be able to access one at any time. Sharing your home and office will become a standard practice. Trading clothing, toys, and tools will be the norm.

Of course, the definition of a resource is open-ended. A resource can be a thing or a service, but it can also be energy, knowledge and ideas. As alternative energy technology advances at an exponential rate, look for more renewables like solar, wind and geothermal—

resources that were previously under-utilized. New Internet platforms will allow expert peer groups to use their collective untapped wisdom and experience to solve the world's biggest problems. At every step, new ideas will emerge to exploit resources that were previously under-used, or not used at all.

This is exciting stuff. If you come up with the right idea, you could make billions. Forget millions, I'm talking about billions. Think about Facebook. What is the core value it provides? It helps people make better use of a previously under-utilized resource: their friendships. They help their members reconnect with old friends and make new friends. What about eBay? They give people a marketplace to sell the stuff piling up in their basement. How about Google? They make available previously hidden knowledge on the web. In each case, they use this new factory value creation strategy. And guess what? Their founders are all billionaires.

Old factory thinkers are themselves under-utilized resources. Stuck in old factories, trying to push out commodity products and services, they don't use all of their skills, knowledge and creativity. They only use a small percentage of their potential.

Don't be one of them. Use new factory thinking to help other people solve their big problems and achieve their big goals. As a result, you'll use 100 percent of your potential and make lots of money along the way. So what can you do to help people optimize previously under-utilized resources?

CHAPTER 15

TOGETHERNESS

Loneliness and isolation are a big problem in today's society. In his book *Bowling Alone*, Robert D. Putnam explained that Americans—and by extension all of us in the western world—have become increasingly disconnected from each other; from our families, friends, and fellow citizens.

A number of factors conspire to make this problem potentially worse. In the old factory era, the mass-market, top-down culture led to regular shared experiences. For example, we watched TV shows at the same time and listened to music on the same radio stations. In most ways, everyone in the culture was synchronized. But in the new factory era, we've become de-synchronized. We select TV shows on streaming services like Netflix whenever we want. We listen to our personal music playlists through earphones while walking down the street. We're in our own little worlds.

Ironically, technology that promised to connect us makes us feel isolated. Social media like Facebook and Twitter gives us a false sense of connection. Text messaging has replaced telephone calls. Staring at a smartphone screen has become the standard way to behave in public and even private settings. I shudder when I see a young mother pushing a stroller: a two-year absorbed in a game on a tablet while the mother listens to music on her smart phone.

Feelings of loneliness and isolation are the digital elephant in the room. Everyone feels it but no one want to talk about it. But this big problem presents a terrific opportunity for you to create new factory value. Bring people together in meaningful ways and you could make a lot of money. (Note: I'm an entrepreneur so I'm always looking for ways to make more money. If you want to do this for other reasons—i.e. create social value, that's great. Go for it. But isn't it even better if you do both: make money and provide social value?)

There are three ways that new factory thinkers bring people together. One, they connect their members together. Two, they connect their suppliers to each other. Three, they connect their members to their suppliers.

In the old factory model, customers did not know each other. The company had a relationship with each customer, but generally the customers did not have relationships with each other. But in the new factory model, the company intentionally creates an integrated community of its members. Being part of this community is seen by members as one of the most important benefits they receive from the new factory. In some cases, it's the primary reason why they signed up as a member in the first place. This is, of course, obvious with social networks, but it also applies to non-technology companies. Consider Harley Davidson. Their customers can join the Harley Owners Group (H.O.G.), participate in local chapters and attend member events. They can also sign up for a weekend ride with other Harley owners. Participation in these H.O.G. activities is very popular. In fact, for most Harley Davidson owners, it's an integral part of the experience.

Creating a membership community like the Harley Owners Group has many advantages for a new factory. You can generate revenue by charging a fee for being a member of the community. Second and perhaps more important, it gives your company greater stability and cohesion. Because your members have a relationship with each other, they're less likely to jump to one of your competitors. If they do, they not only have to sever their relationship with you, they have to sever their relationships with the other members. This is much more difficult and less likely. They may come to dislike your company and yet still stick around because they enjoy their relationships with other members. I have often felt that way about Facebook. Occasionally I've been tempted to cancel my Facebook subscription but I didn't want to break ties with my Facebook friends.

Creating a membership community also helps you get more referrals. When your members feel part of a community, they are more likely to encourage their non-member friends to join. Your members are motivated to contribute to the "network effect" inherent in your community. (The definition of a network effect is: The value of a network increases as more members join the network.) As such, to increase the value they get from your network, they have an incentive to bring more people into the network.

Bringing together suppliers can offer additional benefits to a new factory. In my case, I created an integrated supplier network called *The 10% Referral Club*. For many years, I referred my members to a large number of suppliers. I had negotiated with the suppliers that they would give me a 10% commission for any revenue generated by the referral. I also gave them 10% for any revenue I generated based on a referral from them. While the activity in my one-stop store was satisfactory, it wasn't as active as I desired. The suppliers were not particularly engaged in their relationship with my company. Then it occurred to me to create an integrated supplier network. So I created *The 10% Referral Club*, and invited my suppliers to join. They could now give and get referrals from each other and earn 10% commissions.

The response was swift and positive. The suppliers could see the value of joining the network. They could make money from the community and also feel less isolated and alone. As the new factory community organizer I received the most benefit. My company gained a higher profile and scored a lot of brownie points for setting up the group. But more importantly, it exponentially increased the top-of-mind engagement that my suppliers had with my business. This has led to increased referrals to my company. Better still; as more members have joined *The 10% Referral Club*, the network effect has kicked in, making it easier everyday to attract more new members which generate even more referrals.

The third mode is to bring your members and suppliers together. This is the primary function of the new factory as a value hub. Instead of operating an assembly line to pump out a product or service, the new factory acts as a hub that routes value from suppliers to members, and from members to suppliers. As a value hub, the company sits center stage. It controls the networks and the platform. It sets the structure and policies of the hub. It also stands to receive a portion of the revenue from each transaction that flows through the hub. This is the game being played by new factories like Uber, Airbnb, eBay, Alibaba, and Amazon.

Once you grasp the financial potential of connecting people together, you will be continuously motivated to increase the size of your member and supplier networks. To take advantage of the network effect, you will then be motivated to connect the members and suppliers together. At a certain point, both of your networks will reach a critical mass and they will become self-sustaining.

Once again, take a look around. Ask yourself: Why are platforms like Facebook and Amazon worth billions? Is it because of their intrinsic value as an app or website? No, it's because they have millions of members and suppliers and have connected them together in a network. They also stand to attract even more members and suppliers in the future due to the network effect. That's why investors give these platforms such a high valuation. Investors know there are myriad ways that a new factory can earn additional money from their network communities.

If you're interested in doing this, start immediately. This is a winner-take-all game. Whoever seizes the day first will be the one who benefits from the network effect, leaving laggards in the dust. If you wait, one of your competitors—known or unknown—might organize your community, and then, instead of being the host of the party, you will be merely a guest or shut out all together.

That's also why the first step of the new factory thinking process is to select a type of customer to specialize in. The more specific your customer type, the more likely those kinds of people will coalesce around your platform. For example, if you create a new factory for skydivers over 70 years old, those people will be attracted to your network. But if you pick a customer type that is already taken by another new factory, it is unlikely those people will jump to your network. So don't go head-to-head against an established platform. That won't work. Be original. Find a unique customer type that isn't being served by an existing new factory.

Technology and modern life have pushed us all into our little private pods. In a unbelievably prescient short story written in 1910 called *The Machine Stops,* novelist E. M. Forster painted a bleak picture of a future when everyone lives in a private room and communicates with the rest of humanity through the "machine". The denizens of this compartmentalized world are lethargic, self-absorbed and utterly miserable because they rely on the machine to connect with others. The plot follows the adventures of a young man who yearns to reconnect with the rest of humanity by severing his reliance on the machine. In my opinion that's the point we've reached. While technology has given us amazing benefits in so many ways, it's also driven us apart on a fundamental level.

That's why helping people connect with each other, especially in person, is such an opportunity for new factory thinkers. By providing important emotional value—the desire to connect with others—a new factory can do something meaningful while generating high-profit revenue.

One final note. As the community organizer, you get to decide who gets membership in your networks. You can set the policies, parameters, and membership qualifications. In other words, you don't have to let everyone into your networks. Go for quality rather than quantity. This emphasis will make your networks more attractive to the ideal people you really want.

CHAPTER 16

INTEGRATION

When studying the security failures surrounding the terrorist attacks on 9/11, experts concluded that fragmentation was one of the key culprits. The CIA, the FBI, and the Federal Aviation Administration (FAA)—had not been working together. As a result, vital information that might have prevented the attack slipped through the cracks. This conclusion led to the formation of Homeland Security, designed to coordinate the efforts of the different security agencies.

Fragmentation of this type is a common result of old factory thinking. Each old factory focuses solely on their area of specialization and ignores other parts of the puzzle, assuming that someone else will take care of them. This is a common issue in every old factory industry including financial services, insurance, manufacturing, retail, real estate, distribution, consumer products, and information technology.

Consider Julio Milano. I met Julio following a speech I gave at MIT in Boston for their *Global Entrepreneur Program*. Julio operated an old factory in Columbia that sold security guard services to companies and corporations in Latin America. After hearing my speech, Julio wanted to build a new factory to provide more integrated solutions to his clients.

During our big idea packaging sessions, Julio and I created a program called *The Convergent Security Solution*. In addition to his basic security guard services, Julio would now provide his clients with two new forms of value. To start, he would help them develop a blueprint to integrate all of their security issues into a single system. These previously fragmented security concerns include cyber-crime, counter-terrorism, employee theft, personal security, and data collection and analysis. With the blueprint in place, Julio would then connect his members to his network of security professionals.

Like many old factory thinkers in recovery, Julio initially didn't believe his company could act as an integrator. He didn't think his company had the expertise to provide the additional services. But when he grasped the virtual structure of a new factory and the concept of a value hub, he comprehended how to do it. He would simply bring together outside experts and let them do the work. To assist him in this regard, I introduced him to one of my other members, a cyber-crime consultant. She's one of the world's leading experts in the field boasting the Pentagon as one of her clients. Going forward, Julio simply introduced her company to his members and let them do the work while pocketing a 10% referral fee.

You might ask: What's stopping Julio's members from doing an end run and hiring the cyber-security firm directly? A number of things. One, by acting as a curator, Julio pre-qualifies the quality of each supplier. This saves the members time and effort and increases their confidence that they have a good supplier. Secondly, because Julio begins with a convergent security blueprint, each supplier's work is coordinated with the activities of the other suppliers. This results in a more cohesive security system and puts all of the suppliers on the same page to the benefit of the member.

In his landmark book *The Turning Point*, Fritjov Capra charts how western thought became fragmented. In the 18th Century, scientists and philosophers such as Newton and Descartes visualized the universe as a machine composed of discrete parts. Everything in the universe, they postulated, could be explained by analyzing its separate parts. This way of thinking—a mechanistic worldview—became the underlying operating system of the old factory mindset. Working with this core paradigm, the impulse was to seize on a particular part of the machine and make it your specialty. This had certain advantages such as efficiency and focus, but it also had a huge flaw: fragmentation of thinking and an inability to see the big picture.

Capra encourages his readers to engage in "systems" thinking. Instead of looking at just one part, a systems thinker contemplates the larger system and how all the parts in that system work together. Advances in science over the past 150 years—especially relativity theory and quantum physics—have supported the emergence of this kind of systems thinking in the sciences and humanities. It's now making its way into the business world with the ascendance of new factories predicated on the value of integration.

In another fascinating book *How We Got To Now*, author Steven Johnson explains the serendipitous origins of many great inventions such as glass, refrigeration, electric light, and chlorinated drinking water. His premise is that useful inventions emerge through the integration of previously separate components that converge at a single nexus at the same time. For example, he shows how Gutenberg's printing press converged with advances in glass blowing to set off a flurry of unexpected additional inventions. When books became commonplace, more people realized they were shortsighted, which led to the mass production of reading glasses. The optic advances made possible by the commercialization of reading glasses led to the development of microscopes and telescopes. Microscopes then led to the germ theory of disease, a cornerstone of modern medicine. Telescopes proved the heliocentric theory and led to modern space exploration.

The fascinating examples in Johnson's book point to one underlying principle. The inventors of each innovation were integrators. They didn't invent things from scratch; they brought things together that had been separate. This included the invention of the electric light, the refrigerator, the automobile, the airplane, and the telephone.

By wife Ginny is an inveterate integrator. As a family physician, she's practiced individual and group psychotherapy for more than 20 years. During that time, she's combined elements of Gestalt therapy, Cognitive Behavioral Therapy (CBT), and Mindfulness-Based Stressed Reduction (MBSR) into her own model called *The Mindful Mood Method*. Ever pragmatic, Ginny continually explores the separate fields of psychotherapy to discover if they have ingredients that can be integrated into her ever-evolving model. Her ongoing quest is to use this integrative approach to continuously improve the therapeutic outcomes achieved by her patients.

You too can be an integrator. You can help your customers unify and coordinate their thinking and their actions. Unified thinking will lower their stress and give them clarity. Their actions will be more efficient and less difficult and their lives will be more organized and enjoyable. Mark Landers, a financial advisor, created a big idea called *The Simple Plan Program*. He helps his members pull all of their personal and financial life together into a simple and effective system. He encourages his members to look at their whole life as an integrated system. Each part, he tells them, affects the other parts. A mess in the basement could mean a mess in their investments. A lack of insurance could led to stress, health problems and marital breakdown. A hectic schedule could lead to car accidents and drug abuse. Like Julio, Mark provides new factory value by acting as an integrator.

Once you become an integrator, you realize that one integration leads to another integration. Ken Wilber, author of *The Theory of Everything*, uses the term "nesting" to explain this concept. From his viewpoint, each level of integration nests inside higher levels of integration. Wilbur's body of work is mostly about personal development and consciousness, but it applies equally well to new factory thinking in the marketplace. Individuals and organizations that embrace the highest level of integral thinking will become the overseers of the more limited integral thinkers below them. As I will discuss later, they become the alpha networks that beta networks nest in. That's the game firms like Apple, Google, Facebook and Amazon and a few others are playing right now. Each one is jockeying for position to see who can create the most dominant alpha network. That's why they keep buying up smaller networks. They are vying to create the most transcendent integrated network on the planet.

Ultimately, this principle is simply practical. More integrated solutions are better. They're faster, cheaper and easier to use. They outpace and outperform their less integrated competitors. To play this game, use the new factory thinking process. Ask: Who are we trying to help? What is the big goal we can help them achieve? What is the big problem stopping them from achieving it? How can we bring together fragmented parts to provide an integrated signature solution?

To optimize this strategy, you need to abandon your territorial instincts and question your egocentric ideas of separation. Consider working with your competitors or even enemies to achieve a common cause. Think beyond your industry and get involved in areas you've never dealt with. Enter realms that scare and intimidate you. And most importantly, step back and look at the big picture. Then integrate whatever parts are necessary to provide value to your members.

CHAPTER 17

OBJECTIVITY

In the movie *Miracle on 34th Street*, Santa Claus almost loses his job at Macy's department store when he advises a shopper to go across the street to Gimbels where ice skates are on sale at a lower price. At first Santa's bosses threaten to fire him, but then they realize Santa's objective advice has generated more sales due to positive publicity. More shoppers flood into the store because they see Macy's as honest and objective.

You're not Santa Claus, but you too can benefit from being objective. If you position your company as an honest broker that puts the needs of the customer first you will stand out from your competition. That's because most old factory thinkers don't provide their customers with objectivity. They only want customers to buy their products. They don't want their customers to shop around and they often conceal, or fail to reveal, competitive information that would be in the best interests of the customer.

New factory thinkers, on the other hand, make it a strategy to provide their members with objectivity. They help their customers find the best possible resources even if those solutions come from their competitors. And counter-intuitively this helps them make more money.

Let me give you an example. Bob used to run an old factory that sold life insurance. But it was hard for him to meet new prospects. They thought he was just another life insurance guy pushing policies so he could make a big commission. Many people didn't trust him.

To solve this problem, Bob created a new factory called *The Objective Audit*. He told prospects he would review their current life insurance policies and give them an objective opinion about whether they should keep the policy or get a new one. This service cost $1,500.

Old factory thinkers in the life insurance industry thought Bob was nuts: "No one is going to pay $1,500 for a service they can get from any life insurance agent for free," they scoffed.

But Bob was undeterred. He told them: "They can get free advice from any life insurance agent but they can't get objectivity for free. They know most life insurance agents will advise them to get a new policy because that's how they make their money. But when they pay me $1,500, they have confidence I will tell them the honest truth because they are paying for it."

Over a ten-year period, thousands of clients paid Bob $1,500 for his objective review service. They felt confident that Bob gave them his best advice, not just a sale pitch pretending to be advice. Interestingly, when he advised his members to get a new policy, 90% of them purchased the policy from him even though they could have gone anywhere to get it.

Although Bob's story shows the potential to make money through objectivity, this is still a very difficult concept for old factory thinkers to adopt. They're so used to pushing their products and battling against their competition that they've lost sight of their customers' best interests. But this self-centered approach stops them from seeing a bigger opportunity. If they were to serve as a gateway to all possible resources and solutions, they would attract more prospects and turn them into members. They would then have a much larger number of potential buyers—for both their own products, and those provided by other companies.

There are several strategies to create value through objectivity. One, proactively show your members all of the resources available to them, both from your company and from other companies. Two, develop a separate division that provides coaching and consulting. Operate this new division at arm's length from your traditional products and services. Third, develop supplier relationships with other companies and perhaps even your competitors. If possible, negotiate a finder's fee. (Note: Transparency is important here. Disclose to your members that you receive remuneration from referrals.)

Sometimes old factory thinkers can't get their head around the value of objectivity even when a customer is begging to pay for it. In 1998, our landlord asked my wife and I if we wanted to buy the house we rented. It seemed like a good deal, but we decided to look at other houses before making a decision. We asked a real estate agent if we could pay her $1,500 to show us other houses for sale in the neighborhood. We didn't want to mislead her or take up her time without paying her because we suspected that we would probably buy the house we were renting. But she was adamant that she didn't want us to pay her. She said it wasn't how she did business.

After looking at ten houses for sale, we told her we had decided to buy our existing house. She was upset because she had spent 20 hours and had nothing to show for it. We reminded her that we had been willing to pay for her time. But she couldn't get her head around it. She just wanted to sell us a house. She couldn't see that there was an opportunity to get paid for her advice.

Today, as many traditional products and services become low-margin commodities and sales commissions fall accordingly, many companies now charge fees for their objective advice. In real estate, some brokers now offer a no-commission arrangement, charging a flat fee instead. In financial services, fee-based financial planning is becoming more popular and many property and casualty insurance brokers now provide comprehensive risk management services for a fee.

Consulting and coaching can be much more lucrative because compensation can be based on results not time and effort. For example, if your objective advice helps a person or company save or make a million dollars, it's not far-fetched that they might give you $300,000 or more in compensation. Moreover, they won't care how long it took you to get that result. Even if it only took you one hour, they will still give you $300,000. After all, they have $700,000 more in their pocket because of your objective advice. They won't care how long it took or how hard you worked.

There is one strategy in this regard that is very effective. Tell your prospects they have a choice. They can buy your traditional product or service, or they can enroll as a member in your fee-based consulting program. For the fee, you will provide them with objective advice about what strategies and resources to use. Then tell them they don't need to give up their existing suppliers or advisors to participate in the program. In fact, invite their existing suppliers or vendors to participate.

It's like you're saying: We can be your plumber or your architect. If you hire us as your architect, you can use anyone you like to be the plumber or you can hire us for that too.

Communicating objectivity in this way accomplishes several things. One, when the prospect says they already have a plumber, you can say it doesn't matter. They can keep their plumber. Two, it communicates that your program provides something different and more important than the services offered by a plumber. And three, it positions you as the honest broker that can be trusted compared to the other plumbers who just sell pipes.

I've used this strategy to great effect many times. Recently, a large benefits company contacted me. They were looking to hire a marketing company and wanted me to give a presentation to their executive committee. They planned to have six potential suppliers make a presentation on the same day, one after the other.

I told them I don't do presentations or proposals. Instead I said I would do a free two-hour workshop with them. I also said they could hire me to develop their marketing "blueprint" and then use one of the other firms to implement it. They liked the sound of the workshop but I told them there was one stipulation. I needed to go last at the end of the day.

A few weeks later, I arrived at their office at 3 pm. The executive team looked exhausted. They had sat through five sales presentations. I immediately got them working on their marketing vision. We came up with several amazing big ideas and by 5 pm they were pumped up. I then told them they needed to decide yes or no if they wanted to join my program. I also reminded them that they could hire one of the other firms to implement the projects we would develop. I added it would be important that the other firm—the plumbers— participate in the program sessions. They hired me on

139

the spot.

I got the assignment because I sold objectivity. While the other firms battled it out with each other, I transcended their petty squabbles and incorporated them into my process. During the coaching sessions that followed, the three fellows from the other firm they hired sat at the end of the boardroom looking angry and confused. They were perturbed that I was the client's number one advisor (architect), while they were relegated to secondary status (plumber). They became so unhelpful and obstructionist, the client eventually fired them and hired us to implement the plan. In this way, we got the architect job and the plumber job too.

To provide objectivity, you need to put the welfare of your customers first. Like Santa Claus at Macy's, you may need to refer your customers to your competitors. But this objectivity will attract even more customers to your business and help you make even bigger more profitable sales.

CHAPTER 18

TRANSFORMATION

Fitness is a good metaphor to explain transformational value creation. You could run a fitness club as an old factory thinker or as a new factory thinker. The old factory thinker would provide facilities and exercise programs. The new factory thinker would help its members achieve a transformation in their overall health and fitness. As you'll see, these two approaches are worlds apart.

Most fitness clubs today are run as old factories. They lease space and fill it with exercise equipment. They hire fitness instructors and offer classes such as aerobics, yoga, spinning and weight lifting. Typically, they charge a monthly membership fee competitive with other fitness clubs. So far so good. But the problem is: most people who join fitness clubs don't get in shape. They start off with good intentions but after a few months their commitment wears off and they stop going to the club. Of if they do go to the club, their exercise efforts are haphazard and not part of an overall wellness plan. Of course, a small percentage of the members are self-motivated and get in great shape but the large majority do not. They need more guidance but they don't get it because the club sees its role as a provider of facilities and services. In their opinion, it's up to the customer to make the best use of them.

Fitness-oriented new factory thinkers take a different approach: They provide transformational value. They do whatever is required to help people transition from *out-of-shape* to *in-shape*. They start by thinking deeply and holistically about the problem. Looking at the widest possible pattern they see that many people are unnecessarily overweight, physically weak, and in poor health. They see that the fragmented products and services provided by old factory fitness and health companies are not working together to their fullest potential. To solve this big problem they envision people achieving their ideal weight, becoming stronger and optimizing their wellness by working through an holistic step-by-step transformational process.

New factory thinkers work with the concepts of an *anti-model* and a *model*. The anti-model is a detailed description of how their customers are out of shape. The model is a detailed description of how their customers will be in shape once they have achieved the transformation. The purpose of the new factory is to help its members make the transformation from the anti-model to the model. It facilitates the transformation by bringing together all of the necessary resources, experts, and strategies. It pulls these resources together from different fields. In the case of a fitness new factory, they might use a combination of yoga, nutrition, cognitive behavioral therapy and sleep hygiene to achieve the transformation.

Providing this type of a transformational process can generate more revenue and higher profit margins for a new factory. Sticking with the fitness example, an old factory fitness club might charge $50 to $100 a month for membership, while a new factory fitness transformer could charge $5,000 for their process. Of course, you might counter that no one will pay $5,000, but I disagree. There are plenty of people who will pay for a proper process that works rather than waste money on a fitness club membership they never use or an app that doesn't ultimately achieve the desired result.

Providing transformational value addresses one of the inherent downsides of the old factory economy. Most old factories merely treat problems, they don't cure them. Why? Because old factories don't have an incentive to cure a problem. They make money by continuously treating a problem. Curing it would not be in their best interest. We see this issue in just about every sector of the old factory economy including healthcare, financial services, education, and consumer products.

But new factory thinkers make money by curing problems once and for all. They put aside their former new factory biases, and bring together all the necessary resources and people to make it happen. And they are able to charge higher prices because the value they provide is far superior to the limited and fragmented value provided by their old factory competitors.

So how do you build a transformational process? Let's use the fitness metaphor again. If you want to get people in shape, start by articulating the anti-model and the model. Then plot the first version of the transformation process; what you believe might work. Let's say you outline a nine-stage process called *The Great Shape Formula* that stretches over a six-month period. Then find volunteers to act as guinea pigs and take them through a beta-test of the process. Along the way, learn what works and what doesn't. Based on the trials, take steps out and put other ones in. Reorder the steps and refine how each step is done. Each time you take a person through the process think about how to make it better.

Done in this way, it's inevitable that you will develop an effective transformational process. It might take 10 or 100 iterations, but eventually you will create a polished process that works. You will also have a group of participants who have achieved the model and can testify to the efficacy of the process. At this point, you can start charging premium prices for it.

Once you have your transformational process refined and packaged, you can provide it in many different ways. You can offer it at your fitness club as an additional service. You can license the process to other fitness clubs. Of you can provide it online in a virtual manner and not own a fitness club at all.

The transformational value strategy builds on the other value creation concepts we have already discussed. Your transformational process will achieve better results with less resources (time, money and effort). You will bring to the table resources that are under-utilized such as nutritionists who don't have enough clients or yoga techniques that are rarely taught. You will bring people together, both participants and experts. You will fit together all the pieces of the health and wellness puzzle that are fragmented in the old factory marketplace. You will also provide objectivity. You won't push fitness products and services. You will look for the absolute best solutions even if they are provided by competitors.

Transformational value can be provided in any industry and any type of business. It can be implemented quickly and with little upfront capital. It begins with a clear intention to help others achieve a transformation; to go from being out of shape to being in shape. You can start with one willing participant. Even if you do not yet have all the required resources you can still try to help them achieve the ideal model and realize better results.

Start by thinking deeply about your customers. What is the anti-model they are stuck in? Go into detail. Then imagine the model.

What's is the ideal condition they could achieve? Then think about what's needed to make the transformation from the anti-model to the model. Try out your process on one person. Then a second and a third. Refine the process. Strive to make it better. Then offer the process to your members for a fee.

Once you start thinking in terms of transformations, the value creation part of your brain will light up. You will come up with an endless stream of ideas and strategies. Your thoughts will be more focused, integrated and less scattered. You will know exactly where you are taking your customers and will be better able to explain this aspiration. You will also feel more confident that you can help your members achieve the model.

One last note on this topic. This book is all about transformational value. My big goal is to help you to make the transformation from old factory thinking to new factory thinking. I want you to overcome the old factory anti-model and achieve the new factory model. I am also giving you a process to help you make that transformation.

So what is the transformation you want to help your members achieve?

CHAPTER 19

EMOTIONAL VALUE

As computers and robots take over most of the jobs previously done by old factories, new factory thinkers will provide their members with emotional value. They will make money by transforming negative emotions into positive emotions.

Old factory thinkers rarely consider the emotional state of their customers. The value of their products and services is determined by a rational calculation of their price in relation to the utility of their features and benefits. Granted, advertisers are adept at generating sales by evoking emotional responses but their intention is not to permanently transform the emotional state of their customers.

New factory thinkers understand that the old factory economy, which has focused on providing material abundance, has failed to provide sustainable well-being for the majority of consumers. In fact, studies show that people in wealthy nations suffer high levels of depression, anxiety, feelings of alienation, and other forms of mental illness. It seems that once we reach a certain level of abundance, having more stuff actually makes us less happy. This paradox is expertly explained in a book by John Naish called *Enough: Breaking Free From the World of Excess.* Naish shows that getting and having more things has made many people in our society feel less well emotionally.

"Our race for more and more has born strange fruit: levels of stress, depression

and burnout are all rising fast, even though we live amid unprecedented abundance."

New factory thinkers recognize this big problem and see an opportunity to provide emotional value that cannot be delivered by a computer or a robot. They understand that consumers who are unhappy will pay a lot of money to be happier, especially if this elevated happiness is sustainable.

To create emotional value, start by working with the concept of the anti-model and model discussed in the previous chapter. List the negative emotions your prospects feel when you first encounter them. Do they feel sad, afraid, angry, alone, unfulfilled or frustrated? Do they feel anxious, exhausted or overwhelmed? Then delineate an ideal emotional model you would like to help them achieve. Do you want them to feel happy, safe, peaceful, connected, and fulfilled? Do you want them to feel calm, rested, and at ease? Then brainstorm what resources, experts and processes would aid them in making this emotional transition.

Understanding your customer's emotional landscape requires empathy and an understanding of your own emotions. This kind of emotional intelligence was not nurtured or encouraged during the old factory era. In fact, it was discouraged. Talking about and expressing emotions was seen as inefficient and inappropriate. But in the new factory era, helping your customers improve their emotional state is an opportunity to deepen your relationships with them and grow your business.

The five-part structure of the new factory model inherently provides emotional value at each step. By choosing a specific type of customer (step 1), you demonstrate that your customers are the most important consideration in your business. This makes them feel recognized and supported. By building your business around a big idea (step 2), you demonstrate your understanding of their problems and that you have big goals for them. This makes them feel even more supported and also excited about achieving big goals. By offering free value (step 3), you break through their feelings of distrust and cynicism and build trust. By offering a membership program (step 4), you make them feel special and more confident they will solve their problems and achieve their goals. And by providing a one-stop store (step 5), you make them feel empowered.

Providing emotional value in this manner is one way for humans to compete against the speed and efficiency of computers and robots. While artificial intelligence will be useful in many ways, it is unlikely that it will be able to provide the emotional value that humans can give to other humans. That's why we are seeing a growing demand for social workers, psychotherapists, life coaches, and other mental and physical wellness providers. These emotional value providers go beyond the mere functionality of old factory thinkers and focus on alleviating emotional suffering.

In his book *Hardwiring Happiness*, neuropsychologist Rick Hanson explains that the human brain is wired for three primary emotional needs: safety, satisfaction and connection. Our instincts are to avoid harms, seek rewards and attach to other people. On the deepest level of our being we seek reassurance, encouragement, and warmth. For this reason, a new factory thinker creates value accordingly. She gives her members reassurance that dangers and risks will be avoided. She gives her members encouragement that they will be able to achieve their goals. And she makes her members feel connected in meaningful ways by providing genuine warmth and compassion.

In the previous paragraph, I used a female pronoun because emotional intelligence tends to be a strength among women and a weakness in men. That's why I predict most women will find it much easier to embrace the new factory model than most men, and will achieve much greater success in the marketplace going forward.

So think about how you can provide more emotional value. How can you help your customers or clients feel safer and more secure? What can you do to give them enhanced feelings of satisfaction and fulfillment? How can you help them feel more connected to others?

Some of my program members have embedded emotional value directly into the packaging of their value proposition. They offer three levels of membership. Level one helps their members deal with their risks and threats. Level two helps them achieve their big goals. And level three helps them connect with other members, either online or in person. Prospects can select one of these three choices or start at level one and then proceed to levels two and three accordingly.

If you are not convinced that emotional value creation is an opportunity to make money, consider Starbucks. Why do you think people pay $5 or more for a cup of coffee at Starbucks? Is it because the coffee is better? Unlikely. You can get a good cup of coffee almost anywhere these days. But Starbucks does something better than their competitors. They provide emotional value. When a person buys coffee at Starbucks, they feel special. They feel they are giving themselves a treat. The community atmosphere in the stores also makes them feel more connected. The combination of these emotional value components is the reason why Starbucks customers are willing to pay a premium for a cup of coffee.

Creating emotional value will help your business in many ways. Like Starbucks, if you help your members feel better emotionally, you'll be able to charge higher prices than your competitors. You'll also attract a large number of emotionally-impoverished prospects who are not being served by the old factories in your industry. And you will remain viable and relevant in a marketplace being taken over by computers and robots.

CHAPTER 20

EMPOWERMENT

Back in the late 1970s, I had an experience in journalism school that taught me the value of empowerment. In those days, producing a newspaper was a laborious process with many steps. One of the steps was turning stories written on a typewriting into typeset columns ready for layout. At our school, a woman named Doris operated the only typesetting machine on campus. To get a story typeset, you had to be nice to Doris because frankly she was nasty. Power had gone to her head. If she didn't like you, forget about meeting your deadline. She would either toss your story to the bottom of her in-box or deliberately pepper your story with typos. It was a nightmare.

Fortunately for us journalism students and unfortunately for Doris, the advent of electronic publishing changed everything. Instead of sucking up to typesetters like Doris, we could bypass them all together and create an entire publication ourselves from start to finish with no intermediaries. In journalism, as in many other fields, computers empowered us to take control of our destiny.

Empowering your customers to take control of their destiny is another way you can create value in the 21st Century marketplace. Instead of simply providing products and services, you can create wealth by empowering your customers to create their own products and do their own work.

To illustrate this concept, imagine you're a mountain guide. There are two ways you can provide value to your customers. You can carry them to the top of the mountain or you can empower them to climb it on their own. In the first scenario, you do all the work while the customer goes along for the ride. In the second scenario, the customer does most of the work, but relies on you for your knowledge and support.

My experience in the marketplace indicates that most customers prefer the latter scenario. They don't actually want you to do things for them. They would rather do things on their own with your assistance. That's because a person who accomplishes something on his or her own feels better about the result. They feel empowered.

There are two primary ways to empower your customers. In the first case, the customer does everything on their own. That's why banks give you the capability to do your banking online or through an ATM, and why the oil companies get you to pump your own gas. Downloading work to the customer saves the company money and gives the customer a sense they are saving money too. It is the core strategy behind the success of IKEA for example.

Additionally, the do-it-yourself (DIY) revolution has reached into just about every sector of the economy. Home Depot empowers its customers to do their own renovations. Amazon CreateSpace helps authors publish their own books. And medical equipment companies enable people to take their own blood pressure, monitor their insulin levels, and perform a myriad of other health-related tests without the need to see a doctor.

Advances in technology are fueling the DIY revolution. In their 2006 book *Revolutionary Wealth*, futurists Alvin and Heidi Tofler coined the term *prosumers*; people who act as both the producer and consumer of their own products and services. In the coming years, this trend will continue. Solar, wind and hydrogen technology will empower householders to produce their own energy. 3D printers will empower prosumers to produce their own appliances, clothing, vehicles, and dwellings. Increasingly, you will also see individuals and communities producing and consuming their own food. The opportunity is for new factory thinkers to make money by empowering these prosumers with hardware, software, networked communities, and access to an integrated selection of resources.

The second empowerment strategy is to work in conjunction with your customer on a joint project. In this case, the customer still does most of the work but you are actively involved. Acting as a coach, you guide the customer through a step-by-step process towards the achievement of a big goal. Along the way, you provide tools, offer advice, and encourage them to keep going. While they do most of the work, you are indispensable because they could never achieve the same results without your active involvement.

Assuming the role of an empowerment coach fits into the worldview of new factory consumers. Anti-hierarchical and distrusting of authority, they don't want anyone to have power over them, whether it's an individual, a company or the government. Rather, they want to be empowered and welcome anyone who will assist them in this regard. Let me give you a few examples of how this concept could play out in different industries and sectors:

Healthcare: A new factory healthcare company guides its members through a step-by-step wellness program. It begins with a detailed audit of the member's current health. Together with the doctor/coach, the member develops a personalized health and wellness plan that integrates different elements such as traditional medicine, alternative medicine, nutrition, psychotherapy, and fitness. The member is responsible for implementing the plan and required to meet with the doctor/coach on a quarterly basis. At these review sessions, the member is held accountable for what they have and have not accomplished.

Financial Services: In a financial service old factory, the adviser develops a financial plan for the client and manages their investments. The advisor gets paid an investment management fee and/or earns commissions on the sale of financial products. In a financial service new factory, the advisor acts as a coach and leads a client through a transformation process. Instead of doing everything for the client, the financial coach empowers the client to achieve their financial objectives on their own. The member is given the knowledge and guidance to make the right investment decisions, choose the right insurance policies, stay within a personal budget, and keep track of their cash flow and net worth. In this way, the member takes responsibility for their financial well-being, while the financial coach acts as the catalyst.

Architecture: An old factory architect does most of the work. She meets with a client and finds out what kind of house they want to build. Then she goes away and develops a blueprint. After several meetings with the client, the blueprint is finalized and building begins. A new factory architect on the other hand empowers clients to create their own blueprint. During a "blueprint creation session", the architect/coach uses 3D software to help the client design their own house. Working together, the architect/coach and the client are able to quickly arrive at the desired blueprint, saving everyone time and effort. The client is also happier with the result because they have been an active participant in making it happen.

Business Management Consulting: Old factory consultants provide their clients with advice. New factory consultants walk their clients through a step-by-step coaching process. For example, let's say you are an IT consultant. You begin by teaching your prospects about *The Transparent Logistics Solution*, an IT model you created that helps companies develop supply chain information systems where data is collected and analyzed at every step of the process. By clearly communicating your anti-model and model, you convince a client to develop a transparent logistics system of this nature. As their coach, you give them the tools, strategies and guidance needed to achieve the model. You also make them accountable during monthly progress sessions.

Education: Old factory educators teach classes and courses on specific subjects. New factory educators coach students to achieve their academic and intellectual goals. They begin by helping students develop a vision for their future. They ask the student: What do you want to learn and why? How do you want your education to form you as a person? What kind of career do you dream of? The education coach then helps the student map out a long-term education plan and brings to their attention all of the available educational resources. Over many years, the education coach meets with the student to review their progress, readjust their plan, and present new educational resources that have come on board. In this way, the education coach acts as an objective, high-level academic advisor who ensures that the student makes the best use of the world's fragmented educational resources.

The empowerment techniques used in these examples can be utilized with any kind of customer in any kind of industry or situation. The principles are the same. Instead of doing all of the mental and physical work for the customer, a new factory helps them think about the right things at the right time and take the required actions in the proper sequence. The empowerment coach also ensures that the customer stays on track and makes the best use of the available resources.

It can be difficult to get your mind around the concept of empowerment value because in the old factory era you got paid for your time and effort. The harder and longer you worked, the more money you made. But in the new factory era, you can make even more money by getting your customers to do most of the work. That's because the empowerment model yields better results. Less time is required and the customer gets emotional value from a feeling of personal accomplishment.

So how can you empower your customers? How can you help them climb the mountain on their own? What resources, expertise, and support can you provide to guide them to the top?

CHAPTER 21

CONCEPTUAL VALUE

Hundreds of books have been written on change management by business professors and management consultants, but only one was a bestseller, a little book called *Who Moved My Cheese* by Spencer Johnson. It's the story of four mice who find that their cheese has disappeared from its usual location, never to return. It's a cute tale that teaches a powerful lesson: when things change, you need to accept the fact and look for new opportunities.

Who Moved My Cheese was a global success because it provided conceptual value. The story of the mice gave people an easy-to-remember analogy to use whenever change occurred in their own life: "Our cheese has moved, we need to change too." This concept, packaged as an parable, empowered people to deal effectively with this issue. That's why Johnson's book sold in the millions, and the other more academic books on change management didn't catch on. While they surely contained reams of well-researched data and case studies, the other books didn't empower people to actually do something about change.

That's why conceptual value creation is another massive opportunity for new factory thinkers. It's my conjecture that most added value created in the future will be conceptual. As the world becomes more complex and people are inundated with an explosion of information, images, and ideas, strong communication of clear concepts will be prized and richly-rewarded in the marketplace. New

159

factory thinkers who work skillfully with concepts, metaphors and analogies will stand out from their conceptually-confused competitors.

That's why the big idea is the central component of a new factory. It's not a product or service. It is an integrated package of concepts that captures the imagination of your customers. Clearly communicating the big idea not only helps you attract more subscribers and members, it also provides value in itself.

To explain what I mean, let's pretend you are a manufacturer of electronic components for the automotive industry. Your company has a lot of great customers but you face strong competition from overseas. You are looking for a way to differentiate yourself by providing your customers with added value. You realize that conceptual value might be the answer.

To this end, you develop a big goal: To help automotive manufacturers double their profits. You then identify the big problem: Auto companies do not optimize the electronic systems in their vehicles because they don't entertain out-of-the-box ideas. Your signature solution is to empower auto companies with creative ideas, insider access to best-of-class strategies, and a one-stop store of electronic components from around the globe. You call your big idea *The Inside Innovator.*

But this is just the beginning. You then work out your anti-model and model. You precisely delineate all of the issues that limit the profitability of automakers and identify the core problem, which you title *The Legacy Limitation Trap.* This diagnosis points to the fact that most automakers typically make incremental improvements to their cars year over year, and as a result they fail to make significant leaps in engineering design that could have a huge positive impact. You also fine-tune your model which you call *The Innovation Ignition Model*. The model proposes a new organizational process for idea generation and innovation management in the auto industry.

To communicate your model and anti-model, you take inspiration from Spencer Johnson and his mice in *Who Moved My Cheese* and decide to use an analogy. Because you have a hobby as a magician, you elect Houdini to be your conceptual symbol. You find a picture of Houdini shackled in chains hanging from a crane. This image represents the creative strictures suffered by auto companies caught in *The Legacy Limitation Trap*. You then show another photo of Houdini after he has miraculously liberated himself from the chains. This photo represents an auto company that has embraced *The Innovation Ignition Model*. The analogy is powerful because it points to the universal tension between fundamental polarities: oppression and expression, imprisonment and liberation, rigidness and flexibility.

Armed with your package of conceptual value, you communicate your message through a diverse set of channels. You produce a video, an eBook and an email newsletter. You host webinars and produce a podcast. You give speeches at industry conferences.

Through these efforts you notice something important. Your Houdini concept captures the imagination of your prospects. They are intrigued by your banner showing Houdini in chains with the caption: "Are you caught in *The Legacy Limitation Trap*?" They want to know what it means, and when you explain it, they get it. "That's exactly the problem we have," they say. "We've never thought about it before, but it's true. Our existing design process is limiting our potential." They then invite you to set up a meeting, and over the next year, you help them develop an *Innovation Ignition System* in their companies. This work helps these members streamline their innovation processes resulting in greater efficiencies and more exciting product offerings, both of which boost profits.

This example shows the power of conceptual value. By using the Houdini analogy to communicate a big problem, you get prospects to act on it. You are then able to help them achieve the big goal by empowering them with the needed resources, knowledge and guidance. But the key point is: your skillful packaging of the concept made it all happen. If you had not communicated your ideas well, the prospects wouldn't have understood it, or acted on it. As such, you actually provided your members with most of the value in the first 30 seconds. That's why I say, in the future, as new factory thinkers develop greater conceptual expertise, most of the value in the marketplace will be conceptual in nature. Everything else will be merely implementation.

One way to develop your conceptual packaging skills is to use *The Fork In The Road Method*. Imagine that you are at a fork in a road. Your potential customers are streaming towards you at the fork in the road. Most of them are passing you on the left, which you know is a bad idea. You know that the road on the left leads to a dangerous fall off a cliff. You also know that the road on the right is much better. It leads up a mountain towards a wonderful place called Happy Land. You want to take people to Happy Land, but you realize you have to first stop them from taking the wrong road. So you put up a big sign that says: Stop. Don't Go Over The Cliff. Fortunately, lots of the people notice the sign and stop to talk to you. You explain about the cliff at the end of the left-hand road, and the horrible fate that awaits them if they fall off it. You then explain how wonderful it is in Happy Land.

Using these concepts you empower them with a clear choice: To take the wrong road and go over a cliff or take the right road to Happy Land. And based on your clear communication, a large number of the prospects elect to take the road to Happy Land and hire you as their empowerment coach. As we discussed in the previous chapter, this means they make the climb on their own with your guidance. When they arrive at Happy Land, they are very grateful that you were standing at the fork of the road and did such a great job convincing them to take the right road.

Sadly, many old factories actually help their customers take the wrong road. In fact, the wrong road is lined with vendors hawking their products and services. They don't care if the customer falls off a cliff as long as they make a purchase first. I know this sound harsh, but isn't it true? It's not that old factory thinkers want their customers to fall off a cliff, they just don't see the problem as their responsibility. But that's not what new factory thinkers do. They make money by stopping people from going over a cliff, and they do this primarily by providing conceptual value.

This principle has its roots in the fact that people buy ideas, not products or services. If they like the idea associated with a product they buy it. If they don't like the idea attached to a product, they don't buy. Most of the time, this exchange of ideas and concepts is subliminal. The customer does not know that they are acting on an idea. They think they are making a rational decision. But that's how the marketplace works, even the old factory marketplace. But in the new factory marketplace, this principle is taken one step further.

Ideas and concepts now provide value in themselves. They do not need to be attached to any product or service. The value of the concept is determined by how well it informs and motivates the customer to take the right course of action. This "conceptual empowerment" helps the customer avoid their big problems and achieve their big goals, and along the way motivates them to purchase many products and services.

When it comes to conceptual communication, brevity and precision is key. You need to catch the attention of your prospects in three seconds. You then have 30 seconds to engage their interest. If you still have them at that point, you have three minutes to tell the fuller story. If you haven't captured their imagination after three minutes, you will probably lose them all together. So keep it quick by finding exactly the right words to use. Cut any superfluous details. Get to the point.

Consistency is also important. Once you have a story that works, stick to it. Don't change it because you get bored of telling it. Remember that every person is a new audience. They haven't heard your story before, and they need to hear the story that works.

So think about the fork in the road your customers are approaching. What is the wrong road? What happens when they go over the cliff? What is right road? What is it like in Happy Land? Then work on explaining these concepts in the most effective way possible. Use metaphors and analogies. Hone your language. Use interesting images. Be bold. Take chances.

CHAPTER 22

INTERFACES

My company Bishop Communications, which I started in 1987, was built on the foundation of an interface: the Apple Macintosh desktop operating system. Based on a GUI architecture (graphic user interface), the Mac was a vast improvement on the green screen DOS-based computers that preceded it.

Until the Mac came along, computers did not inspire me. They were just a step up from a typewriter. But the Mac interface empowered me. I could see dozens of ways I could make money from it: specifically electronic publishing. I could create newsletters and magazines from start to finish, all on the Mac screen. Emboldened by this interface, I quit my job and started a publishing business.

Over the years, the emergence of other interfaces also empowered me. A technology called FirstClass enabled me to create a second company to provide bulletin board systems (BBS) to corporate clients. The World Wide Web interface spawned scores of lucrative business opportunities, and the iPhone OS interface changed the way I do business.

These experiences taught me that interfaces in themselves create value. They also make their inventors a lot of money. Consider these interfaces: YouTube (videos), Facebook (friends), Google (search), and TripAdvisor (travel reviews). These interfaces, and many like them, are popular because they provide an easy and pleasant way to do something useful. They also organize and simplify the management of information.

New factory thinkers understand that the company that creates the best interface wins. They know that consumers are fickle and impatient. If a new and better interface comes along, they know their customers will jump ship in a jiffy. So they take the creation of interfaces very seriously. That's why even Google has to maintain strict control over their home page (a minimum of text, lots of white space), and continuously upgrades the power of their search algorithms. Even the king of search could be usurped by a better interface.

There are two kinds of interfaces that a new factory thinker can create: machine-based and human-based. A machine-based interface resides online and is accessed by the consumer using their computer or other device. A human-based interface involves live human interaction between the interface agent and the customer. Either way, they perform the same function. Whether machine or human, the interface makes it easier for the customer to get things done.

As the world explodes exponentially with new information, new technology, and new ideas, the demand and need for interfaces will rise accordingly. We need interfaces to manage our money, our health, our time, our relationships, our hobbies, and our businesses. We also need interfaces to manage all of our interfaces.

Take passwords for example. Back in the 1990s, I had one or two passwords to remember. Now I have over a hundred for all of the services I use on the Internet. To manage them, I subscribe to LastPass. After logging into LastPass, it automatically logs me into all of my other sites. This save me time and I don't have to keep all the passwords in my head. As a result I feel less stressed. (Note: While I was writing this book, hackers attacked Lastpass. This security breach was disconcerting, but I continued to use the service because the interface is so pivotal in my work.)

Designed as a value hub, new factories are interfaces by default. Customers come to a new factory to access a galaxy of resources, either online or by dealing with a human being. The better the interface provided by the new factory, the more members it attracts and the more repeat business it generates. This has been my experience with Amazon. They provide me with a one-step buying process called One Click. Once I find what I want, I simply click a button and the process is done. They already have my credit card and my shipping address. Their publishing interface is also sublime. Working on their CreateSpace interface, I can publish a book, including this one, with ease. The process takes 90% less time than the traditional publishing process and costs 75% less.

Of course, you might not yet have the resources to develop an interface like Google or Amazon, but that's okay because you can act as a human interface. You can help your members deal with complexity and enable them to get things done quicker. You can be their trusted advisor and a one-stop source for information and assistance.

I have many people in my life who act as an interface for me. At home, I have an assistant who handles 99% of my household chores. Whenever we have a problem with our house, like a leaky roof, I get her to source a contractor to solve the problem. I don't have to know, or want to know, the details. At my cottage, I have a fellow who acts as my rural resource interface. Whenever there is a problem, like a collapsed tree, I call him. With a minimum of communication he ascertains the issue, finds a contractor and gets the job done. I also have a team of people at my office who also act as interfaces. I tell them that they are my complexity catchers. Their job is to catch complexity before it reaches me. As a result, they free up my time and energy to do my job; coaching members and writing books like this one.

So become an interface for your customers. Make their life simpler and more organized. Become the single source they seek out whenever they have a problem or need something. Make it easier for them to get things done. Be more helpful than anyone else they've ever met. Catch their complexity. Be indispensable. (Note: Being an interface does not mean you have to be a doormat or a slave. It's not necessary for you to be available 24-7. You can set your boundaries.)

In the book *Lean Startup*, Eric Ries chronicles a step-by-step method for developing an effective interface. He suggests that you begin with a concierge stage where you do everything manually using human-to-human contact. Then you slowly migrate functions and activities online while reducing the company's human involvement. In this incremental fashion, the interface evolves based on what works and what doesn't.

We used this method for a personality test we created called *The Trumark Index*. Once we had developed the first version of the questions, and the schema for the personality profiles, we tested them on 100 live subjects and created the reports manually. Based on this experience, we fine-tuned the questions and began to slowly automate the reporting function. They we created an interface so the subject could complete the test online. Ultimately, we arrived at an effective interface for the test that is completely automated.

Once you start thinking in terms of interfaces, you will see many business opportunities that were previously obscured by old factory thinking. You'll see how you can create better interfaces for your company, both online and in person. You'll also see how you can create an interface for your whole industry, or even beyond your industry.

Like conceptual value, interface value is a packaging exercise. The best online interface is a dashboard or portal that masks infinite complexity. It turns something disorganized and fragmented into something simple and elegant. This is the premise behind the success of Uber for example. It provides a simple interface to order a taxi. It displays how far away the cab is and when it will arrive. It shows you the name of your driver, and the estimated cost of the trip. It also keeps track of your trips and how much you paid. You can also rate the drivers and they can rate you. The transaction is then concluded automatically because the system already has your credit card. That's why Uber contends it's a technology company, not a taxi company. It merely provides an interface that is better than what came before.

So start thinking about interfaces. Where is there an opportunity for you to create a new interface? If you come up with the right idea, you could make billions.

CHAPTER 23

TEACHING

There's an old expression: He who can does, he who can't teaches. But in the new factory marketplace, this aphorism is turned on its ear: He who can gets paid a wage, he who teaches gets rich. This updated saying points to a universal truth; what you know is much more valuable than what you do.

That's why new factory thinkers become teachers. They teach their prospects and customers what they have learned from their experience. What they've learned works and doesn't work, and the best ways to solve big problems and achieve big goals.

Old factory thinkers don't see teaching as their role in the marketplace. In fact, they don't believe teaching is a good idea. They jealously guard everything they know. They keep their wisdom and knowledge under lock and key. As one businessman told me: "If I teach people what I know, what would they need me for?" This objection is understandable, but it misses the bigger point: If people see you as a valuable source of knowledge and wisdom, they will be attracted to you and keep coming back for more of the same. You will become a leader and an expert in their estimation.

As we've discussed in previous chapters, empowering people to do things themselves is an effective value creation strategy in this marketplace. People today don't want you to have power over them; they want you to empower them. And the best way to do that is to empower them with knowledge and wisdom. If you do that, you will not only attract more subscribers and members, you'll also have greater influence in their lives and their businesses. As such, they will more likely join your membership program and buy products and services from your one-stop store.

Most old factory thinkers also don't believe they are experts. Sure, they have educational credentials and business experience, but they direct this knowledge to the task of pumping more products and services through their assembly line. New factory thinkers, on the other hand, recognize the value of their knowledge. They don't set themselves up on a pedestal, but they realize that they have important information to share with the world. They also see that teaching is a great opportunity to get more members and make more money.

The first step is to take what's in your head and get it down on paper (or some electronic equivalent). Write down the top 10 tips you have for your customers. Here are some example tips:

- Create a mind map of ideas before you start writing a story
- Stop using electronic devices one hour before going to bed
- Drink five liters of water each day
- When brainstorming, do it in small groups and then bring them together to share their ideas at the end
- Use a proactive maintenance schedule to cut downtime by 35%
- Stand, don't sit, while having team meetings

There are a million possibilities. When you start listing your tips, you will realize how much you know. Over the years, you've learned hundreds of things that don't work, and a dozen or so things that work every time. It is valuable information. It can help people avoid all of the trial and error you went through. It can save their health, their relationships, their businesses, even their lives. That's why it's really your duty to share it.

Just one technical note here. When you make your list of tips, start with a verb, such as create, start, drink, do, use, stand. Also give the tips as if you are teaching them how to do it themselves. Don't say: Hire us to help you... or hire an expert to... Those are self-serving tips that border on selling, not teaching. In addition, try to create original tips that your audience hasn't heard before. Don't just regurgitate tips from books by other experts. Your audience has probably read those books too.

When you have your 10 tips, add meat to the bone. Write one page to further explain each tip. Then turn these 10 pages into an ebook. Create a blog, video or podcast about each tip. Run a seminar or webinar. Write an article for an online magazine. Give a keynote presentation. Write a full-length book.

As you further hone and expand on your tips, you will better appreciate the usefulness of your knowledge, for your audience, and for yourself. Your audience will be empowered with information they can use. As for yourself, you will feel more confident and clear about what you know, and be positioned as a pre-eminent teacher and thought-leader in your field.

You will also realize that there is no danger is sharing everything you know. In fact, the danger is that you don't share it. That's because someone might come along and beat you to the punch. They will become the recognized expert on your subject, not you. You will then be subjected to the unpleasant experience of sitting in an audience while one of your competitors gives a keynote speech you could have given. That will drive you crazy.

By sharing your knowledge, you will attract more people into your sphere of influence. Sure, some of these people will take what you teach them and do it themselves, but they would have done that anyway. But you will also reach a larger number of people who appreciate what you're saying, get it, and want you to help them implement your ideas.

In addition, investigating and articulating what you know, you find even more hidden knowledge in your cranium. You also see the world more clearly and pull in additional information from the environment. That's the thing about knowledge. It shrivels up when it's not shared, and expands exponentially when it is.

In the new factory marketplace, knowledge is infinitely more useful than effort. You can make a lot more money teaching what you know than doing something for someone. Not sure? Consider this. You can get paid for cutting lawns, for let's say $20 per lawn. If you cut five lawns in one day, you make $100. You could also hire five employees and cut 25 lawns a day for a total of $500 a day, less labor and operating costs, for a net of let's say $200. Under this old factory model, there is a limit to the amount of money you can make, and to scale it, you would need to buy a lot of lawn movers, and deal with a lot of complexity. You would also face significant competition from other lawn maintenance companies.

A new factory lawn company would take a different track. They would become teachers. They would teach people how to maintain their own lawns. They would teach them about the different kinds of grasses, the best way to fertilizer them, and how to water them. They would create a website called *The Lawn Academy* and offer videos and courses on lawn care. They would also set up a one-stop store where lawn and garden companies could sell their wares, and even sell the services of other lawn care companies. They could also set up an accreditation course for lawn care providers to become *Lawn Academy Certified*.

In this example, the new factory is built around teaching as its core value proposition. Most of this teaching is provided as free value in order to attract subscribers and members, who then purchase additional products and services from the one-stop store. And by attracting thousands, perhaps millions of lawn owners, the new factory also attracts a lot of suppliers who are willing to give The Lawn Academy a portion of each sale. Even more compelling: the old factory lawn care company might reach a few hundred customers while the new factory Lawn Academy could reach millions.

The great thing is: Teaching is a way to sell without selling. As we discussed earlier on, consumers today are hard to reach with a sales pitch. But if you have something useful to teach them, they will put down their armor and engage in what you are saying. They will see you as an expert, not a salesperson, and hold you in much higher regard. Moreover, the cost of being a teacher has dropped almost to zero. It costs virtually nothing these days to produce blogs, videos, podcasts, books and webinars. It also costs nothing to spread your knowledge through social media.

Understanding that you are an expert with a lot of valuable knowledge to share is a key step towards becoming a new factory thinker. In the old factory, no one cared about what you knew. They just wanted you to keep the assembly line moving. But in the new factory marketplace, you can step back from the machine and look at the big picture. You can see what's actually going on. From this perspective you can recognize patterns that are hidden when standing at the assembly line. You can see the big problems that are not being solved by old factories. You can also see problems that are being caused the old factories. And you can see the potential to achieve much bigger and better goals, and new ways to achieve them. You then have inexpensive tools to teach people what you've learned.

You also need to realize that you understand your customers better than they do in many ways. They are caught up in their own little worlds, but you have worked with hundreds of people like them. You see the patterns of commonality. You see that they all have the same problems, and deal with those problems in the same ineffectual ways. You can also see their future. You know what happens to people like them if they don't address their big problems. You also know what is possible if they do. Once again, your knowledge and wisdom is extremely valuable. So don't waste all of your energy and spirit in simply pumping products and services through an assembly line. Become a new factory thinker: Teach.

One final note on this topic. The most important activity of a new factory thinker is to think. The key is to think about the right things. Direct your thinking outward towards the problems and opportunities your customers have. Think deeply about the barriers that are stopping them from achieving their big goals. Think about the best ways for them to achieve these goals and when you are ready, share your insights.

One second final note: New factory thinkers regularly step away for extended periods of contemplation. They balance being active with being thoughtful.

CHAPTER 24

CURATING

The Internet gives us access to an ever-growing amount of information, options, and resources, but it also creates a big problem: How do you find the quality gems among the rabble of rubble?

Certainly technology helps. Google and other search engines present a list of options but you're still left to do most of the work yourself. For example, let's say you need a lawyer. A search engine will turn up lawyers in your area, but how do you know if they're any good? You might turn to a friend, but they might only know one or two lawyers. Or imagine that you're looking for a good CRM (customer relationship management) system for your company. Search engines display hundreds of options, but how do you know which one will best suit your company? It will likely take you many hours of trial and error to test and select the right one.

But what if you could work with a curator who has done all of the research and legwork for you? Wouldn't it be useful if there was a curator of lawyers who has spent 10,000 hours interviewing and vetting law firms. Would you be willing to pay the curator money if they could put you in touch with exactly the right lawyer for your needs? Perhaps you would. What about the CRM system? What if you could speak to a CRM curator who has tested out every system, and rated them by functionality, ease of use, and cost? Would you be willing to pay this curator to save you a hundred hours of effort and ensure that you get the best CRM system for your needs? Perhaps you would.

These two scenarios illustrate why curation is another value creation opportunity in the new factory marketplace. As more options and information become available in every field, it's harder than ever for the layperson to find the best solution for their needs. That's why we need curators more than ever.

So what exactly is a curator? When you hear the word, you probably think of a librarian or someone who runs an art gallery. You're right, they're curators. The librarian directs you to the best books to read. The art gallery owner directs you to the best art. They're valuable because they have taken the time, and have the expertise, to separate high quality from low quality.

In the old factory era, the goal was to increase quantity. More stuff. More experiences. More possibilities. But in the new factory era, the goal is to increase quality. Better stuff. Better information. Better experiences. In this environment, if you want quantity, use technology. If you want quality, use a human being, a curator. To see what I mean, consider these three scenarios:

Curator Scenario 1: You're a cancer survivor. For five long years, you dealt with the cancer healthcare system. You know first hand what works and doesn't work when it comes to dealing with cancer. Now that you're healthy, you decide to become a cancer care curator. You create a new factory called *Cancer One*. When someone becomes a member of your *Cancer One Program*, they meet with you to discuss their options. You point them to the right resources and away from the wrong ones. You explain how to deal with the various private and public institutions. You point out insurance issues and how to cut through red tape.

Providing value as a curator, you save your members time, money, and effort. You provide emotional value because you help them avoid unnecessary stress and worry. By directing them quickly to the best-quality options for them, they get the help they need faster. It is not incredulous to postulate that your role as a curator increases the chances they will survive their cancer ordeal.

Curator Scenario 2: You love fishing. Over 20 years, you've been to more than 400 fishing spots around the world. A lot of them were really bad but a few dozen were amazing fishing holes that few people know about. So you decide to turn your passion for fishing into a new factory called *Far-Flung Fishing Adventures*. For a membership fee, you direct people to your curated fishing holes and advise them on the best way to get there, where to stay, and how to catch the fish. You teach them in a few hours what took you 20 years to figure out. They save time and money and enjoy the best fishing adventures in the world.

Curator Scenario 3: You're a management consultant. You have read more than a 1,000 business books. You decide to provide curation value by starting a new factory called **The Laser Library**. You help your members zero in, like a laser, on exactly the right knowledge they need from all of the business books out there. Acting as a curator, you save your members time, money, and effort, by delivering the exact high-quality information they need to grow their businesses.

The re-emergence of curators like the three mentioned here is a certainty in the new factory marketplace. But this time, the curators will charge a fee for their curation services, rather than making their primary revenue from the sale of products and services. You see, that's what went wrong over the past 30 years. Curators lost their jobs because they didn't get paid for being curators, and as a result, the marketplace didn't respect the value of their insider knowledge.

But now, many consumers realize acting as their own curators is time-consuming and doesn't always work. They realize finding the cheapest hotel online isn't the same as finding the best hotel for their needs. They realize that peer-to-peer opinion services like TripAdvisor are often unreliable and time-consuming. They realize nothing can replace a human being who has been there and done that. Only this time, they will need to pay the curator for their expertise.

Like in the case of teaching, technology is also making it easier for new factory thinkers to provide value as curators. It's easier than ever for curators to find options to evaluate and then to communicate the best selections to their members.

So think about providing value as a curator. There are a million possible things to curate such as: alternative energy systems, child care facilities, motorcycles, pets, fertility clinics, footwear, nightclubs, apps, hot tubs, pilgrimage sites, anti-terrorism methods, hot sauces, aggregate companies, self-help books, watches, underwear, forms of government, or kites. You can curate anything. It's what the marketplace needs. It could also be a lot of fun.

CHAPTER 25

ENTERTAINING

In the new factory marketplace, you have new competitors: talking cats and celebrity bloopers on YouTube. These entertainments, along with movies, music, TV shows, sports, and video games, compete with you for the attention of your prospects.

That's why you need to have more fun with your customers. You don't have to put on a clown nose or start tap dancing but you do need to inject a three-finger shot of entertainment into your business. Otherwise, you'll commit the biggest sin of the new factory era; being boring.

In their book *The Experience Economy*, Joseph Pine and James Gilmore explain that having fun with customers is a powerful way to add value and differentiate your company. When I read it in the 1990s, Pine and Gilmore's book was revelatory to me. I had never thought of my business as a show, like putting on a play. But it made sense so we enacted several changes to improve our customers' experience. We scripted our process from start to finish, and we made our show more entertaining. I remember joking that it needed to be a comedy, not a tragedy, and preferably a romantic comedy, where the customer not only loves us, they also have a good laugh.

Our new approach worked because it observed one of the key marketing principles that states: "People buy more when they're having fun." This axiom is true because when people have fun they put down their guard, open up and trust you more, which makes them more likely to buy. That's why I write books with titles like *How To Sell A Lobster* and *The Problem With Penguins*. By having a little fun, often at my own expense, people are more receptive to my message.

In the old factory era, fun was frowned upon in the workplace. It was okay to have fun after work and on the weekend, but business was serious. No joking around on the assembly line. Laughter and joviality got in the way of productivity. Moreover, the top-down hierarchical organizational structure of old factories didn't lend itself to hilarity and good times.

But times have changed. The new factory structure is non-hierarchical. People want to have fun at work, and your customers want to have fun too. The lines between work and play are now blurred. Acting too serious, which old factory thinkers believe portrays gravitas and professionalism, are now interpreted as stuffiness and authoritarian. It's a turn off.

So it's a good idea to have a little fun with your customers. You don't need to overdo it. A smidge of fun will do. One of my clients put a picture of an ostrich on her website with a caption that read: Don't bury your head in the sand. Deal with your safety issues today. The quirky picture worked. It got prospects laughing and thinking: "Yup that's us. We're ostriches. We've buried our heads in the sand." My client credits this dollop of ostrich fun as the key reason that her business fortunes improved.

Another client of mine gives celebrities a silver dollar wrapped in bubble wrap. She tells them that their money is fragile; that most celebrities blow all their money. She tells them she will "bubble wrap" their money and protect it. This fun bubble wrap metaphor has helped her attract dozens of celebrities to her business. They call her the "bubble wrap lady".

Another client starts his process by helping his clients make a bucket list of all the things they want to do before they die. This fun exercise differentiates him from the other boring financial advisors in town and serves a practical function. Once prospects have done the bucket list, they are more motivated to create a financial plan and invest their money.

Another client gives his members a special perk. If they sign up for his program, they get a key to a wine locker at the best restaurant in town. When they eat at the restaurant, they can open the locker and drink the wine inside for no charge. He tells me that his members love the wine locker perk. "I'm convinced," he says, "the primary reason some of them sign up for my program is because they get a key to the wine locker. "

Another client, a used car salesperson, gives his customers a hug. He has become Canada's huggable car dealer. This fun hook has made him a household name and increased his sales. "Some people come into our dealership just to get a hug," he says.

These examples show that adding entertaining value isn't hard. You just have to try it. You have to take a risk. But you'll learn that the biggest risk is not having fun. After all, if your competitors offer an experience that's more fun than yours, you will lose customers.

In addition to fun, you should make your customers' experience more enjoyable than your old factory competitors. Traditionally, dealing with old factories was not enjoyable. It wasn't much fun to visit a bank or dentist. They weren't even trying to make it fun. But now, for example, TD Bank, one of the leading Canadian banks, uses the slogan: "Banking can be this comfortable." TD Bank is trying to distinguish itself from its less comfortable competitors. They realize "comfort" and "enjoyment" are emotional values that customers crave.

Doing something unexpected is another way to provide fun. Mix up your process. Do things differently that the standard in your industry. Bring in unexpected guest experts. Send your members a board game after a stage in your process. Send an electronic reward when they complete a task of your coaching process. Call them on Monday morning to invite them to a members-only party. Shake things up. Surprise them.

Another trend that is taking hold in the new factory marketplace is gamification. Leading companies have turned their marketing campaigns into games. Using apps and social media, they get their prospects and customers to play a game that relates to their business. Nike, for example, has a running app that tracks your runs and challenges you to run faster and longer. When participants advance through a level, they receive badges or credits. The whole experience of interacting with the company is a game that customers love to play. It also keeps them tied to the company—through fun and entertainment.

Old factory thinkers are generally a serious lot. They think business is business. It's serious. But now, being serious might be a liability. Having fun might be a lot smarter.

SECTION FOUR

NEW FACTORY FOUNDATIONS

CHAPTER 26

VALUE HUBS

Karl Marx was right about a few things. In his economic theory, he conjectured that societies organize themselves around their "means of production". The means of production has two parts: raw material and the technology used to increase the economic value of that raw material. In an agrarian society, the means of production consists of soil (raw material) and the shovel or plow (technology). In an industrial society, the raw material is human labor and the key technology is the assembly line. Marx believed that class warfare was inevitable because the owners of the technology (capitalists) exploited the providers of the raw material (the workers). What Marx didn't foresee was the new factory.

The central premise of this book is that the means of production in our society has changed fundamentally. It now consists of thinking (the raw material) and networked communication (the technology). This change in the means of production has transformed the marketplace on a fundamental level. It is now possible for everyone to be the master of his or her own means of production. To do this, however, we must rewire our minds, and reorganize how we provide value in the world. We must relinquish assembly lines and become value hubs.

When you act as a value hub, you help your customers achieve their big goals and solve their big problems. Your intention is to get the job done by providing whatever resources are necessary, even if another company or industry provides them. Instead of trying to pump out a pre-determined product or service, you route a stream of value to your customers and capture wealth in the process. Constantly shifting and adapting, you develop new ideas and source new resources depending on the ever-changing needs of your customers. To stay resilient, you develop an operational structure with minimal fixed assets, and as much as possible your operation is virtual.

By "routing" value to customers, a value hub mirrors the physical structure of the Internet itself, where information is sorted and distributed by routers connected together in a network. The routers take incoming fragmented information "packets" and directs them to their destinations where the packets are reassembled and presented in the form of emails, web pages, videos, voice-over-Internet, and a myriad of other forms.

As the Internet and its networked structure has become the dominant means of production in our global economy, the marketplace and our society have increasingly come to resemble it. Companies and individuals who use new factory thinking and operate as value hubs are more successful because they have organized their thinking and operational methods to match the new means of production. Old factory thinkers who continue to operate like assembly lines are now realizing less success because their thinking and methods are not congruent with the new means of production.

Old factory thinkers will be further marginalized because the structure of their operations (assembly lines) won't fit into the networked structure of the emerging new factories. It will be like trying to stick a square peg into a round hole. New factory thinkers, however, will connect seamlessly into the growing network of value hubs, where each person and company will route value to and from each other.

It's important to stress that, even though the Internet is the means of production driving the emergence of value hubs, it does not mean that a value hub needs to be technologically-driven. It does not. A value hub is primarily driven by its intention to help customers achieve their big goals and solve their big problems. How this is accomplished requires much more than just technology. It requires the intention to put your customers' goals ahead of your own. It requires objectivity and a willingness to innovate and continuously create new kinds of value. You also have to be willing work together with others, perhaps even your competitors. These requisites of a value hub are not technology-dependent. In fact, a new factory thinker does not tie her value hub to any particular technology because she knows that technology is constantly changing.

Most old factory thinkers resist the value hub concept. They are heavily invested in their products and services and have significant capital tied up in their assembly lines. They are also supported in their opposition by the old-factory-industrial-complex including old factory politicians, bureaucrats, media, banks, energy companies, and large corporations. But their resistance is futile. New factories and their value hubs are going to rock their world and it's going to happen faster than they can imagine.

Alpha Hubs

As new factories become more powerful and the value hub economy gains steam, some new factories will become "alpha hubs". They will have the most members and route the most value through their hubs. Smaller new factories will become suppliers to these dominant players as "beta" hubs. Companies that continue to operate as old factory assembly lines will be marginalized or disappear altogether.

This is the game being played by new factories like Apple, Google, Facebook, Twitter, and Amazon. They're battling it out to see which one will be the globe's premier alpha hub. That's why they're buying up other new factories and developing new value components like driver-less cars, home automation systems, and cloud-based services. They want a greater and greater share of their members' transactions to go through their hub.

Fortunately, you don't need to be a big company like Apple or Google to play this game. You can become the alpha network in your particular customer niche. For example, if your customer type is mountain bikers, you can try to route more mountain bike-related value through your hub than any other company in your industry. That's why new factory thinking is such an opportunity. Anyone, anywhere, can become an alpha hub. You just have to pick a customer niche that no one has captured yet. Typically, the first new factory to exploit the network effect with an untapped customer niche will hold an unbeatable advantage over also-rans. This game is winner-take-all.

Instances

Another concept that is critical to new factory thinking and the value hub paradigm is the idea of "instances." This term points to the fact that your customers' needs are unique for each specific instance of time and place. In other words, what your customers need in one instance may not be what they need in another instance. Their requirements change year-to-year, day-to-day, minute-by-minute.

For example, you might have a health-oriented new factory that serves adult children of parents who suffer from dementia. You have a value hub that provides a constellation of products and services for this market. But you also know that the needs of your members change constantly. As such, you have a team of coaches who are skilled at investigating the particular needs of members at each instance of contact and empower them to provide mass customized solutions.

Mass Customization

Providing unique "packets" of value for each "instance" is another feature of a new factory, and why new factory thinkers build value hubs that facilitate mass customization.

An old factory is designed for mass production. Its goal is to efficiently deliver the same product or service over and over again. But in a new factory, the goal is to efficiently provide a unique solution over and over again. Let's look at it this way. An old factory auto company would build an assembly line to produce the same car every five minutes, while a new factory auto company would create a value hub to produce a unique car every five minutes. In fact, it might produce a car in one instance and a lampshade in the next instance. The key point is: The new factory would provide this type of mass customization just as efficiently as the old factory because it is configured to do so. It is designed from the bottom up as a value hub.

Mass customization is what the market wants. Your customers' needs change continuously. Each instance is different. If you aren't able to meet their unique needs in an instance, your customer will turn to a new factory that can. And if they do leave, your competitor will become the alpha network instead of you.

Thinking is the new raw material

Thinking is the most important activity in a value hub. A new factory thinker is always contemplating how to solve her members' big problems and achieve their big goals. She continuously hones her model and anti-model, and looks for new strategies, ideas and resources. Most importantly, her thinking is directed first towards the needs of her members, not her own.

That's why this book is called The New Factory "Thinker". We have reached the point in human economic history when thinking is the primary raw material in our economy. How we use our minds will determine our individual success and the future of our society. From my perspective, our minds are an untapped resource. We aren't using them for the right purposes, and as a result, we aren't achieving our full potential. But when we see our companies and ourselves as value hubs, we naturally engage in the right kind of thinking and achieve our full potential.

Connecting The Value Hubs

One businessman asked me: "But what if everyone builds a new factory and creates a value hub? Won't that negate my competitive advantage?"

His question stumped me for a second. But I knew he didn't have anything to worry about because most old factory thinkers will never create a new factory. Most of them will ride their old factory train over the cliff.

But I had a better answer. "That will be great," I said. "Each value hub will connect to every other value hub. We will share our members and resources with each other."

Since I gave that answer, I've become more convinced that this is what will happen. Each value hub will connect with the others, in the same way that all computer devices are now connected by the Internet. It will commonplace for new factories to give and get referral commissions from other new factories. It will be a win-win for everyone. It will also dramatically increase the efficiency and frequency of economic activity.

So don't delay. Build your new factory now. Then connect with other new factory thinkers. Route value from your company to their value hub and vice versa.

Imagine the possibilities.

CHAPTER 27

IDEAS

Ideas are the energy that drives a new factory. New factory thinkers are always looking for ideas to help their members solve big problems and achieve big goals. They have a core concept—a big idea—as the central foundation of their business. This big idea is independent of any product, service or technology so it's not vulnerable to changes in market conditions. No matter what happens in the future, the new factory's big idea is immutable.

New factory thinkers understand that consumers buy ideas, they don't buy products and services. When considering a purchase, they make their decision based on the idea attached to the product. If they like the idea they buy it. If they don't like the idea, they don't buy it.

Consider Costco. Their success is based on a big idea: Our members save money by buying in bulk. That's why Costco sells so much stuff. Their "members" are driven by an idea in their mind: "I'm saving money by buying in bulk. The more I buy, the more I save".

I'm sure you've heard the slogan: Whatever happens in Vegas, stays in Vegas. This is another example of a big idea. It plants the idea in your mind that you can go wild in Las Vegas because no one will find out back home. You are free to have a good time. Las Vegas uses this idea to differentiate itself from its competition. There are thousands of casinos around the world, but there is only one Vegas.

It's important to point out that consumers don't necessarily know they have a big idea in their mind. It might be subliminal, but it still drives their behavior. Moreover, most old factory thinkers don't know the idea they are projecting into the marketplace. They are not thinking on the level of ideas. They simply sell based on the features, benefits and price of their product.

That's why new factory thinkers are more deliberate about the big idea they attach to their business. They aren't just trying to create a slogan or catchphrase; they use a big idea as the foundation of their business. As we discussed earlier, a big idea has three primary components:

• The big goal you are trying to help your customers achieve;
• The big problem you are trying to help your customers solve; and
• The signature solution you use to achieve the big goal and solve the big problem.

When you communicate these concepts, your customers form an idea about you in their mind. The objective is for them to see that you are doing something new, better, and different that takes everything to a much higher level. With this idea "package" in their minds, your customers see you as distinct and superior to the competition.

In addition to the three primary big idea components, new factory thinkers also try to project these ideas:

- Our business is all about you, not us
- We're experts, not salespeople
- We're trying to help you achieve your goals
- We're not just trying to sell you our products
- We're objective
- We're doing big things and we want you to you come along for the ride
- We're always on the leading edge
- We're fun

Remember that the big idea is all about the customer and aspirational in nature. It's what you're trying to help your customers become. For example, you might try to help them:

- Win a gold medal at the Olympics
- Become ten times healthier and more fit
- Achieve academic excellence
- Enjoy a wonderful life
- Strengthen their relationships
- Be a good steward of the environment
- Achieve inner feelings of contentment
- Develop their artistic and creative skills

Note that your big idea is a suggestion. You are suggesting a big goal for your customers to pursue. The strategy is to get them excited and inspired to do something big. You then help them refine the idea and make it more specific to them. For example, your big idea might be to help people enjoy their life 20 times more. You then help your members define what the big idea would look like for them such as: To play golf every day, or to spend more time with grandchildren.

In the new factory future, most value will be delivered with ideas. Properly packaged and communicated, big ideas will warn people of dangers they don't know they have, and inspire them to achieve goals they never thought they could. Ideas will bring people together and give greater meaning to their lives. They will also keep people focused and committed.

In the old factory era, productivity and efficiency were considered to be the keys to success. But in the new factory era, big ideas will be more important. Supporting and nurturing big ideas will be the primary activity. Children will be taught from a young age to brainstorm, prioritize and implement big ideas. Governments will make big idea creation their top priority. And the companies that develop the best big ideas will be the most successful.

So what's your big idea?

CHAPTER 28

WEIGHTLESS

Everyday in the new factory future, the weight of the economy will get lighter and lighter. For each unit of value delivered, the weight per unit will fall until it is virtually weightless.

We are already seeing this trend. The weight of the equipment needed to deliver movies, music and newspapers has dropped precipitously due to the digital revolution. Appliances and consumer electronics have become lighter as quality and functionality has increased. Companies that used to host their own data servers now use the cloud. Everywhere you turn, the trend is towards lighter, better, virtual.

Many old factory thinkers still equate their stuff with success. The more stuff their company has—buildings, desks, trucks, computers—the more successful they feel. But new factory thinkers have a different idea—they strive to get rid of as much stuff as possible; to become weightless.

Weightless new factories run circles around heavy old factories. Consider Uber. How much does that company weigh? A lot less than the taxi companies because Uber doesn't own any taxis. Their drivers own their own cars. Uber doesn't own them, and they don't want to.

What about Airbnb? How much does that company weigh? Not much. What about Google, Amazon, eBay, Apple, and Facebook? They don't weigh much either. But they are all worth billions. How come? Because they are new factories that have made it their strategy to minimize the weight of their companies.

Your customers don't care if you have an office, desks, trucks or manufacturing equipment. They just want value from you and they don't care how you do it. Gone are the days when a fancy office or a fleet of trucks would impress customers because they know the cost of this stuff is included in the cost of the product. They are now more impressed that you can deliver value faster and for less money by running a weightless, virtual operation.

Going weightless saves you money but it also drives you toward value creation. As you shed fixed operational assets and use outside resources on an as-needed basis, your company becomes more value driven. You spend less time dealing with operational issues and more time helping customers. You are also more nimble because you're not tied down to a lot of stuff.

Several years ago, I had a vision for a weightless company. At that point, I had a large team of employees, two offices, lots of desks and computers, and regular migraine headaches. Everyday I came into the office to face another operational issue. The photocopier was broken. An employee was sick. Light bulbs were burned out. The computer server had crashed.

I had had enough. I wasn't having any fun and I wasn't making enough money. My monthly fixed overhead was huge, and worst of all, I had little time to help my clients work on their big ideas. It was apparent that the heavy weight of my company was stopping me from delivering maximum value to my customers.

So I decided to go weightless. Over a three-year period I helped my employees find other jobs or set them up with their own businesses. I got rid of all the desks, servers, and telephone equipment. Everything must go was my motto.

My weight-loss program was exhilarating. Every time I got rid of something I felt liberated. My migraine headaches became less frequent and I felt more relaxed. I also had more time to concentrate on my clients and their big ideas.

That was the most interesting part. Getting rid of stuff forced me to think: What is the core value I actually provide to my clients? What are the things we do for them that are superfluous? What can be provided by other suppliers? The answer was obvious: big ideas. The most valuable thing we delivered was big ideas. Everything else was just busy work that could be delivered by someone else. And the cool thing was, I didn't need a ton of stuff to give someone a big idea.

Today, as I write this, I still have an office. I need a place to meet my members. But it is a much smaller space. I don't need rooms and rooms for all my old factory stuff. The nice thing is: I'm spending less money, but the space is much nicer and in a better location.

As for staff, they are all virtual. I have a virtual assistant who takes my calls and books my appointments. She works from home, about 50 kilometers from our office. My head graphic designer lives 300 kilometers away. I also have a virtual team of 30 other suppliers, some of whom live on the other side of the world.

Losing all that old factory weight makes me feel ten years younger. I have more time to work on big ideas with my members, and because I'm not dealing with so many operational issues, I have more time to enjoy my life. I'm also able to work anywhere. Yesterday, I worked at a Starbucks. The day before that I worked at the library. And today, I am working at home in my kitchen. I'm less tied down and more freed up. And by the way, I doubled my income because my revenue has remained steady while my overhead has been cut in half.

In some ways, my business diet was a lifestyle choice. I wanted a better life from my business. But it was also the right move because the new factory marketplace is rewarding the light and punishing the heavy. Lighter companies are more competitive and flexible. They can provide more value at better prices. That's why every heavy old factory must be on the lookout for weightless competitors. The lightweights are going to run rings around them.

Here are ways you can make your company less heavy:

- Use cloud-based virtual services
- Let your employees work at home
- Get rid of any stuff in your business that does not provide value to your members
- Get smaller, but better office space, or get rid of your office all together
- Weigh your briefcase. Figure out how to drop its weight by 50%
- Scan and digitize all documents, including archived documents
- Get rid of filing cabinets.

A great book that is helpful in this project is called *The Life-Changing Art of Tidying Up* by Marie Kondo. Marie suggests that you hold each object in your hands (if you can) and decide if it gives you joy. If it doesn't give you joy get rid of it. If it does give you joy, keep it. You could replace joy with value. Only keep things that provide value to your customers.

Granted, I've got a small business. I'm also an entrepreneur. I can move a lot faster than bigger companies. But entrepreneurs like myself typically respond more quickly to market trends. If we don't we go broke fast. That's why I see this trend towards weightlessness coming to every industry and every business. It's what the marketplace is dictating. Due to market conditions, light companies will beat heavy companies in the coming years. So eventually, every successful company will be virtually weightless.

Consider Four Seasons, one of the most successful hotel chains in the world. They don't own most of their hotels. They license their brand and their systems to people who actually own the buildings. Four Seasons knows that owning hotels is risky and capital-intensive. They make their money by providing value to guests, and let others carry the weight. Four Seasons is virtually weightless.

Instead of trying to amass lots of physical stuff, work on accumulating intangible assets such as:

- subscribers, members, and suppliers in your networks
- renewable membership fees
- trademarks and domain names
- proprietary systems and programs
- online services and systems

Whenever possible use resources owned by other companies. Let them assume the costs and risks. In the new factory era, owning the old factory means of production is not the way to make money. Machines and other industrial equipment quickly become obsolete and their maintenance also requires a lot of time and attention that cannot be directed at creating and providing value.

So start losing weight. The lighter the better.

Special note: The issue of outsourcing is a touchy subject in some circles. Entrepreneurs are supposed to create jobs not eliminate them. But the marketplace is not idealistic. It wants what it wants. That's why jobs will be replaced by work. In the new factory future, there will be less jobs, but more work. Companies with less full-time employees will be more successful and will generate more wealth. They will then be able to hire more people to do more work. But these workers will not be employees. They will be new factory entrepreneurs who operate as a value hub. These new factory entrepreneurs will have more freedom and make more money than old factory employees.

That's why politicians and the media need to stop talking about job creation, and start talking about value creation. Otherwise people, especially young people, will waste years looking for a job, when they could spend their time building a new factory.

CHAPTER 29

SLOW

If you have read my book *How To Sell A Lobster*, you know I worked as a waiter while studying journalism in college. It was an entrepreneurial job because I could earn bigger tips by giving added value to my customers. One way I did this was to ask them a simple question: Would you like your dinner fast or slow?

Some patrons wanted it fast: They needed to get to a movie in 45 minutes. Other customers wanted it slow: They were celebrating a special occasion—like a birthday or an anniversary—and wanted to take three hours.

This single question doubled my tips. I gave the fast customers speedy service and they left me big tips. I took my time with the slow customers and they also gave me big tips. The other waiters, however, gave everyone the same speed of service, about 90 minutes from start to finish. They got smaller tips because the fast customers missed their movie and the slow customers felt rushed on their special occasion.

This experience taught me that some customers want things fast and other customers want things slow. That's why I suggest your new factory have two divisions: fast and slow.

During the old factory era, speed and efficiency were the primary objectives: Speed up the assembly line and produce more products faster and faster. This accelerated productivity certainly increased profits and standards of living, but it also led to certain downsides.

Our lives sped up. We now rush through our days trying to get more and more accomplished and suffer stress and burnout as a result. Being in a hurry, we don't pause and contemplate what we're doing. We rarely slow down to look at the big picture, set clear goals, or create a better plan for the future.

New factory thinkers acknowledge this big problem and offer their customers an opportunity to slow things down. They offer a choice: fast or slow. If a customer wants a product or service fast, they do a quick transaction. If a customer wants it slow, they provide a comprehensive step-by-step process. In the first case, the fast customer gets what they want: fast access to products that are competitively priced. In the second case, the slow customer gets what they want: The time and attention of a caring human being at a premium price. It's like the difference between a fast food restaurant and a gourmet restaurant.

It's likely you already have an old factory that provides fast access to products and services at competitive prices. I had one client tell me: "My insurance brokerage is the best hot dog stand in town. I'm just not making enough money because all of my competitors sell the same hot dogs and the margins keep dropping."

I suggest you keep running your old factory. Keep selling your customers hot dogs if that's what they want. But also build a new factory to offer slow gourmet services at premium prices. You will be surprised to discover that many of your customers will be willing to pay you a lot of money for your gourmet program. Relatively speaking, it's like the difference between getting paid $3 for a hot dog and $300 for a gourmet meal.

So what would you offer your customers as a gourmet meal? For starters, the gourmet meal needs to be slow. You will spend many hours with them and give them your complete attention. During this time, you will do many of things we've discussed in this book. You will provide free value by teaching them about their big problems and the big goals they can achieve. If they join your membership program, you will do your signature activity with them. You will help them create a blueprint to achieve their big goals and empower them with the resources in your one-stop store. You will also meet with them regularly to keep them on track, and over time, help them achieve a transformation.

This type of slow program provides your members with tremendous value. It gives them an opportunity to deeply contemplate what goals they truly want to achieve. It helps them create a long-term plan, keeps them working towards their goals, and achieve better results using less resources. Slow also gives them significant emotional value. They feel more relaxed and confident. They feel safer and more supported. They feel more fulfilled and connected. They also have greater peace of mind that everything will be okay. That's why slow members are willing to pay you $300, instead of $3. They get so much more.

Let me stress one point. Not every prospect will be willing to pay $300 for your slow program. It might only be one out of ten, or one out of a 100. But that doesn't matter. The people who sign up for your slow program will be much more profitable than the customers who buy your hot dog. Eventually, you will have a large roster of gourmet members and be able to close your old factory hot dog stand if you want.

In the old factory era, wealth was created by going faster. The faster you moved, the more money you made. So everything and everyone sped up. But now the gains made by going faster have reached a point of diminishing returns. It has created such an over-abundance of supply that most products and services have become low-margin commodities. Fast has also turned us into the slaves of our machines, and because the machines are speeding up at an exponential rate, we can't keep up.

In the new factory marketplace, slow is the new fast. As the economy evolves into an interconnected network of value hubs, more value will created with less effort. It will no longer be necessary to create wealth by going faster. You will create more wealth by going slower. By taking the time to contemplate, think and be creative, we will create a society that is much calmer and prosperous.

So slow down.

CHAPTER 30

TRANSCENDENCE

Once upon a time, a queen and king were building a castle but the project was beset by delays and cost over-runs. Things got so bad, the royal couple decided to visit the job site. When they arrived, they saw two men working in a ditch. They asked the first man: "What are you doing?" and he replied: "I'm digging a ditch. I'm the best ditch digger in the kingdom." Then they asked the second man the same question and his answer surprised them: "I'm helping to build your castle and I have some ideas on how you can build it faster, better and for less money."

Impressed, they told the second man to put down his shovel and climb out the ditch. "So what are your ideas?" they asked. For next twenty minutes, the second man shared his observations, ideas and recommendations. When he was done, the royal couple hired him as their castle-building consultant.

Six months later, after the castle had been built on time and on budget, the royal couple threw a party to celebrate. In appreciation, they asked the second man to attend. At the party, they introduced him to other queens and kings and recommended his services. "Without him, this castle would have never been built," they said.

Over the next ten years, the second man helped build 30 other castles. He was heralded as the best castle builder in the kingdom. In the process, he became a wealthy man and built his own castle.

One morning, the castle builder decided to take a trip into town. Riding in his carriage, he noticed a crew digging a ditch by the side of the road, and then he recognized his former co-worker, the first man, laboring away with his shovel. Covered in dirt and sweat he looked old and exhausted. The castle builder could hear his friend boasting to the other workers: "I'm the best ditch digger in the kingdom."

So what's the moral of the story? What's the difference between the first man and the second man? Why did the first man stay stuck in the ditch, while the second man became a rich and famous castle builder?

The second man was a new factory thinker. He looked at the big picture. He knew his job wasn't just about digging ditches; it was also about building castles. Even in his lowly role as a ditch digger, the second man understood his job's greater purpose. As such, he looked up from the ditch and thought about ways to help his customers, the queen and king, build their castle better. With this perspective, he focused his intellectual and creative capacities and came up with a stream of value creation ideas. Then opportunity knocked and he was ready.

Using new factory thinking, the second man transcended his initial position to assume a higher role that was more lucrative and more fulfilling. He made the transition from low-end value based on time and effort, to high-end value based on ideas, strategies and results. He also went from doing something that just about anyone can do to providing value that is rare. All of these factors made him more successful.

Most people have the potential to build castles but they settle for making their money by digging ditches. Hard at work in the ditch, they forget why the ditch is being dug in the first place. The ambitious ones then make a further mistake. They try to be the best ditch digger. It's a mistake because even the best ditch digger can only make so much money. And in most cases, the customers don't care if they're the best. In their mind, ditch diggers are a dime a dozen.

That's why I wrote this book. I want you, and everyone else, to achieve your full potential. I want you to make the transformation from a ditch digger to a castle builder. But first, you have to realize it's possible, and then rewire your mind. You have to start thinking about castles, not ditches.

The second floor

One way to get out of the ditch and achieve transcendence is to occupy the second floor. Think of it this way: Imagine that all the competitors in your industry are at a trade show. Each company has their own booth. They talk about why their products and services are better, but as far as the customers are concerned, all the vendors are basically the same. The only difference is price.

Because you're a new factory thinker, you use a different strategy. You keep your booth on the trade show floor, but you also get some space on the second floor. The good thing is: you're the only one up there. When a prospect comes to your booth, you invite them up to the second floor. You say: "It's quieter up there. We can take the time to get to know each other. We've also got some ideas on how you can do things better."

On the second floor, your prospect calms down. You have a great discussion. You find out their current problems and goals. You then explain the big problems the customer doesn't know they have and get them excited about the big goal. Then you say: "We can work with you on the second floor—at a higher level—and then you can go downstairs to hire a supplier on the first floor, either us or one of our competitors."

This story illustrates the power of transcendence. By taking everything to a higher level, you stand out as one-of-a-kind. You also engage the customer at a higher level. They see you as a caring expert not just a vendor or salesperson.

When you take up residence on the second floor, you also see the marketplace more clearly. You see all the ways that the old factories on the first floor are not serving the full needs of their customers. This gives you ideas on how to fill those needs. You also see how you can make money by working in collaboration with your competitors on the first floor.

Being on the second floor also makes you feel better. You use more of your knowledge, skills and talents. Your work is more fulfilling. It's also more meaningful because you help people deal with bigger problems, achieve bigger goals, and achieve bigger transformations.

So what's stopping you? Stop digging ditches. Build castles. Stopping fighting it out with your competitors on the first floor. Take some space on the second floor. Transcend.

CHAPTER 31

WELL-BEING

Old factory thinkers operate from the equation: More consumption equals more happiness. New factory thinkers use a different equation: *Increase well-being using less resources.*

In the new factory era, everything and everyone was focused on production and consumption. As machines, assembly lines and production processes became more efficient, the world prospered. People made more money and bought more stuff. Millions of people were lifted out of poverty and became, if not rich, at least middle class. No longer living on a subsistence level, many people were happier. The old factory equation worked.

But now the old factory equation doesn't work as well as it used to. Every industry is crowded with old factories selling the same things. Computers and robots are replacing human labor. And many consumers, who have all the stuff they need, have discovered that material abundance doesn't meet all their needs for happiness.

In this environment, trying to make more money by selling more stuff will be very difficult. You can only make so much money selling hot dogs. That's why you need to look for new ways to provide value that take everything to a much higher level. And the highest level of value is well-being.

Well-being is the ultimate form of value because it's what every human being wants on a deep level. From the moment of conception, we seek comfort, love, connection, and peace of mind.

But somewhere along the way, old factory thinkers forgot about well-being. Caught up in a whirlwind of production and consumption, they lost sight of the point. Just like the ditch digger who forgot about the castle, old factory thinkers forgot about well-being.

The old factory era driven by the consumption of resources was a good start, but it wasn't the end of the story. It was stage one. The new factory era, driven by value hubs, is stage two. Increasingly, we will witness an increase in well-being; physical, intellectual, and emotional as new factories invent novel ways to deliver it. The overall consumption of resources will fall while well-being-driven economic activity will increase.

Let me be clear. The drive towards an economy and marketplace driven by well-being is not an idealistic wish. It's the inevitable result of market forces. Consumers seeking well-being will create a demand to be met by enterprising new factory thinkers out to make a profit. That's why the emergence of the new factory era is so exciting. It will not be driven by ideology; it will be driven by market forces.

Using the ideas and strategies presented in this book, start your new factory today. Seek to help your customers achieve greater well-being using less resources. If you have good intentions, and want to help people, you will figure out the best way to do it.

So don't delay. Start building your new factory right now.

CHAPTER 32

THE NEW FACTORY FUTURE

Down in the ditch, locked in old factory thinking, lots of scary notions can come to mind about the future: What if competitors offer a lower price on ditch digging? What if technology replaces human ditch diggers? What if the demand for ditches dries up?

When these worries about the future crop up, old factory thinkers try to shrug them off and keep digging. If we just work hard everything will turn out okay, they say to themselves.

But new factory thinkers don't worry about the future. They see where the world is headed and they embrace it. They feel confident because their new factory is designed to provide value no matter what happens in the future. Instead of worrying about competitors, they transcend and collaborate with them. Instead of fearing technology, they use it to empower themselves and their members. And instead of worrying that demand will dry up, they create demand by bringing new, better, and different big ideas to the marketplace.

Indeed, a new kind of world is approaching faster than most people imagine. Exponential growth is happening in many fields. In the next few years, look for the emergence of cheap solar energy connected to smart grids, driver-less cars, and the Internet Of Things. New forms of currency will emerge. 3D printers will transform manufacturing. Other advances in medicine, transportation, communications, and genetic engineering will come fast and furious.

These changes, and others that are unforeseen, will transform our society on every level. How we relate to each other will change. What we think and believe will change. And how we work will change.

There will be profound disruption. Millions of jobs in old factories will be lost. But new factory thinkers will prosper and create a new kind of economy. The wealth they create will dwarf the wealth created during the old factory era.

It's my belief that new factory thinkers will build a better world for everyone.

It's my hope you will be one of them.

Bill Bishop

SECTION FIVE

APPENDICES

ACKNOWLEDGEMENTS

Giving birth to the ideas and strategies in this book would not have happened without the assistance of many midwives. First of all, I want to thank my wife Ginny McFarlane. She gamely puts up with my problematic persona and creative peccadillos (of which she is all too familiar). Without Ginny, I would not be a new factory thinker and there would be no new factory book. At the office, I get amazing support from a terrific team including Sonia Marques, Corey Kilmartin, Nancy Smith, Nona Lupenec, and Stephen Lindell. For their life-long encouragement, I also want to thank my sister Diana Bishop, my son Douglas Bishop, and my stepdaughter Robin Schulman.

Finally, I want to express my gratitude to the many new factory thinkers in my BIG Idea Adventure program. By adopting, testing, and refining the new factory model, they have demonstrated true leadership in their industries. They are: Nate Sachs, Harold Agla, Bob Kowaleski, Greg Barnsdale, Raymond Rupert, Tyler Trute, Allain Labelle, Lordy Numevekor, Doug McPherson, Jim Moniz, Owen Smith, Rick Bauman, Stephen Gregory, Mark Wadey, Frank Karkowsky, Hugh MacDonald, Jerry Brown, John Pedhirney, Tullio Andreis, Debbie Abdool, Brian Cavell, Carol Lagasse, Joe Hollen, Mette Keating, Donald McDonald, Caroline and Mark Marrs, Charles Brophy, Peter Lantos, Murray Malley, Peter Milnes, Harold Mertin, Robert Kleinman, Howard Cadesky, Christina Cheung, Dan Conway, Claude Jeanson, Wade P. Walters, Charles Martin, Jim Lorence, Scott

Wallschlaeger, Dave Baily, Bev & Brian Jeffray, Wesley Forster, Wayne Mcleod, Fritz Steigmeier, Gillian Rivers, Steve Meldrum, Ron Pennington, Ray Senez, Peter Boys, Peter H Minerson, Mark Melvin, W.W. (Bill) Cormylo, Alan Waters, Dan Pisek, Jim Holland, Holly Eburne, Heather Wilson, Bruce Cappon, Leland H. Pilling, Barry Pascal, Mark Rich, Glen Seeman, Michael Capesky, Randy Johnson, John Firstbrook, Michael Sgarbossa, Matt Chrupcala, Rob Cima, Sean Gooden, Richard P. Harvey, Robert Mackwood, Byron Woodman, Lee McGowan, Kelly Taylor, Richard J. Price, Matthew J. Grace, Richard Rhodes, Ralph Van Winkle, Robert Gignac, Brock T. Jolly, Mark Church, Ryan Bosch, Van Luong, Jennifer Black, Eliza Fok, Richard Sheppard, Lee Williams, Tom Johnson, Eric Jozsa, Edward Jermakowicz, Danny Antidormi, Adam Wyrcimaga, Dawn Gordon, Robert Kostynyk, Yvonne Martin-Morrison, Mitch Silverstein, Don Tharp, Richard & Sheila Gane, Andy Wimberly, Martin DeArtola, Jeff Calibaba, Robert Young, Thomas E. Snell, Mike Goldman, Stephen Lomsdalen, Bob Nigol, Jim Coleman, Jody Samuels, Malcolm Silver, Nancy Youngs, Brian Kroeger, John Vandeweerd, Judi Smith, Julio Milano Kishel, Joel Cadesky, Laura Lomow, Joe Macartney, James Hill, Nancy Hall, Jaime Nolan, Karen Gurland, Jim Frye, Michael Gibson, Robert Moore, Don Walmsley, Jeff Anderson, Merri Macartney, Hugo Lozano, Dione Spiteri, Taylor Thoen, Reinier van Elderen, Danish Naeem, John Dehart, Ruth Gerath, Steve Steinman, Nick Bloor, Abhijeet Narvekar, Meaghan Guisti, John Brick, Marianne Cherney, Susan Keshen, David Marinac, Ned Vedo, Sheila Goldgrab, Ken Ramsay, John Connell, Theo Kowalchuk, Jim Perchaluk, Dinis Prazeres, John McDonald, Bruce Frick, Aaron D. Lieberman, Dustin Addison, Joshua Rudolph, Oliver Keller, Nicky

Billou, Michael Palmer, Paul Stadnick, Sam Cellini, Mike Evers, John Ardill, James Hill, Luke Kratz, Bill Simpson, Russ Culver, Sheldon Waltman, Bernard Weinstein, John Carter, David Eason, Chris Hotze, John Keeler, Brad Jenkins, Rick Caouette, Mark Stempel, Cindi Scafide, Jim Durkin, Frances Toler, Elizabeth Schwarzman, Kerry Wallingford, Paul Elmslie, Jeremy Fulford, Gordon Reid, Fleur M. Sluijter, Ramon Solinas, Mark Hudon, Mark Landers, Glenn Fabello, Mike Greenwood, Marcelene Anderson, Christine Butchart, Carlos Valiente, Greg de Koker, Fred Hann, Garnet Clews, Patrick Power, Jeff Kropman, Glen Ronald, Derek Wiens, Michael Brown, Rick Hyde, Marty Levy, Renato & Eva Degasperis, Chris Miller, Catherine Vu, Helen Lopez, David Wu, Nathan Kupusa, Ryan Mitchell, Sarah Cato, Emile Studham, Kaela Bree, Sunny Verman, Gerard Murphy, Evelyn Jacks, Debbie Hartzman, Rob Eby, Helena Pritchard, Jody Steinhauer, Grant McPhail, Mike Giokas, Evan Giokas, Mark Humphrey, Wayne Wilson, Mark Calla, Jim McGovern, Pat Carroll, Jeff Wachman, Debbie Voth, Dennis Graham, Rod Vatcher, Nicole Amies, Dave Pettigrew, James P. Gunn, Tim O'Toole, Frank Wiginton, Rona Birenbaum, Ben Katebian, Merv Peters, Carien Jutting, Enjoli Brown, and Jeff Wachman.

BIBLIOGRAPHY

Anderson, Chris. *Free: The Future of a Radical Price*. New York: Hyperion, 2009. Print.

Anderson, Chris. *The Long Tail: Why the Future of Business Is Selling Less of More*. New York: Hyperion, 2006. Print.

Berger, Warren. *A More Beautiful Question: The Power of Inquiry to Spark Breakthrough Ideas*. N.p.: n.p., n.d. Print.

Bishop, Bill. *Beyond Basketballs: The New Revolutionary Way to Build a Successful Business in a Post-product World*. Bloomington, IN: IUniverse, 2010. Print.

Bishop, Bill. *Global Marketing for the Digital Age*. Lincolnwood, IL: NTC Business, 1999. Print.

Bishop, Bill. *Going To The Net: Winning The Psychological Game Of Tennis*. New York: Amazon, 2014. Print.

Bishop, Bill. *How to Sell a Lobster: The Money-making Secrets of a Streetwise Entrepreneur*. Toronto: Key Porter, 2006. Print.

Bishop, Bill. *The Problem with Penguins: Stand out in a Crowded Marketplace by Packaging Your Big Idea*. S.l.: Iuniverse, 2010. Print.

Bishop, Bill. *The Strategic Enterprise: Growing a Business for the 21st Century*. Toronto: Stoddart, 2000. Print.

Bishop, Bill. *Strategic Marketing for the Digital Age*. Lincolnwood, Chicago, Illinois, USA: American Marketing Association, 1998. Print.

Brynjolfsson, Erik, and Andrew McAfee. *The Second Machine Age: Work, Progress, and Prosperity in a Time of Brilliant Technologies*. N.p.: n.p., n.d. Print.

Capra, Fritjof. *The Tao of Physics: An Exploration of the Parallels between Modern Physics and Eastern Mysticism.* Berkeley: Shambhala, 1975. Print.

Capra, Fritjov. *The Turning Point.* New York: Simon & Schuster, 1982. Print.

Carr, Nicholas G. *The Glass Cage: Automation and Us.* New York City: W.W. Norton, 2014. Print.

Catmull, Edwin E., and Amy Wallace. *Creativity, Inc.: Overcoming the Unseen Forces That Stand in the Way of True Inspiration.* N.p.: n.p., n.d. Print.

Cialdini, Robert B. *Influence: The Psychology of Persuasion.* New York: Collins, 2007. Print.

Diamandis, Peter H., and Steven Kotler. *Abundance: The Future Is Better than You Think.* New York: Free, 2012. Print.

Diamandis, Peter H., and Steven Kotler. *Bold: How to Go Big, Achieve Success, and Impact the World.* N.p.: n.p., n.d. Print.

Diamond, Jared M. *Collapse: How Societies Choose to Fail or Succeed.* New York: Viking, 2005. Print.

Dixon, Matthew, and Brent Adamson. *The Challenger Sale: Taking Control of the Customer Conversation.* New York: Portfolio/Penguin, 2011. Print.

Doidge, Norman. *The Brain That Changes Itself: Stories of Personal Triumph from the Frontiers of Brain Science.* New York: Viking, 2007. Print.

Duhigg, Charles. *The Power of Habit: Why We Do What We Do in Life and Business.* New York: Random House, 2012. Print.

Eggers, William D., and Paul Macmillan. *The Solution Revolution: How Business, Government, and Social Enterprises Are Teaming up to Solve Society's Toughest Problems.* N.p.: n.p., n.d. Print.

Ferriss, Timothy. *The 4-hour Work Week: Escape 9-5, Live*

Anywhere, and Join the New Rich. Chatham: Vermilion, 2011.
Print.

Flynn, Anthony, Emily Flynn. Vencat, and Dennis C. Flynn.
*Custom Nation: Why Customization Is the Future of Business and
How to Profit from It.* Dallas, TX: BenBella, 2012. Print.

Friedman, Thomas L. *The World Is Flat: A Brief History of the
Twenty-first Century.* New York: Farrar, Straus and Giroux,
2005. Print.

Godin, Seth. *Permission Marketing: Turning Strangers into Friends, and
Friends into Customers.* New York: Simon & Schuster, 1999.
Print.

Haidt, Jonathan. *The Happiness Hypothesis: Finding Modern Truth in
Ancient Wisdom.* New York: Basic, 2006. Print.

Hanson, Rick, and Richard Mendius. *Buddha's Brain: The Practical
Neuroscience of Happiness, Love & Wisdom.* Oakland, CA: New
Harbinger Publications, 2009. Print.

Hanson, Rick. *Hardwiring Happiness: The New Brain Science of
Contentment, Calm, and Confidence.* N.p.: n.p., n.d. Print.

Harnish, Verne. *Scaling Up: How a Few Companies Make It ... and
Why the Rest Don't.* N.p.: n.p., n.d. Print.

Hawken, Paul, Amory B. Lovins, and L. Hunter Lovins. *Natural
Capitalism: Creating the next Industrial Revolution.* Boston: Little,
Brown, 1999. Print.

Heath, Chip, and Dan Heath. *Made to Stick: Why Some Ideas
Survive and Others Die.* New York: Random House, 2007. Print.

Heath, Chip, and Dan Heath. *Made to Stick: Why Some Ideas
Survive and Others Die.* New York: Random House, 2007. Print.

Heath, Chip, and Dan Heath. *Switch: How to Change Things When
Change Is Hard.* New York: Broadway, 2010. Print.

Howe, Jeff. *Crowdsourcing: Why the Power of the Crowd Is Driving the*

Future of Business. New York: Crown Business, 2008. Print.

Isaacson, Walter. *Steve Jobs.* New York: Simon & Schuster, 2011. Print.

Johnson, Steven. *How We Got to Now: Six Innovations That Made the Modern World.* N.p.: n.p., n.d. Print.

Kondo, Marie, and Cathy Hirano. *The Life-changing Magic of Tidying Up: The Japanese Art of Decluttering and Organizing.* N.p.: n.p., n.d. Print.

Kurzweil, Ray. *The Singularity Is Near: When Humans Transcend Biology.* New York: Viking, 2005. Print.

Lanier, Jaron. *Who Owns the Future?* N.p.: n.p., n.d. Print.

Levitt, Theodore. *Marketing Myopia.* Boston, MA: Harvard Business, 2008. Print.

Lewis, David. *The Brain Sell: When Science Meets Shopping: How the New Mind Sciences and the Persuasion Industry Are Reading Our Thoughts, Influencing Our Emotions and Stimulating Us to Shop.* N.p.: Nicholas Brealey, n.d. Print.

Lietaer, Bernard A., and Jacqui Dunne. *Rethinking Money: How New Currencies Turn Scarcity into Prosperity.* San Francisco: Berrett-Koehler, 2013. Print.

Lowitt, Eric. *The Future of Value: How Sustainability Creates Value through Competitive Differentiation.* San Francisco: Jossey-Bass, 2011. Print.

McLuhan, Marshall. *The Medium Is the Message.* Corte Madera: Gingko Pr., 2005. Print.

Marchal, Lucie. *The Mesh.* New York: Appleton-Century-Crofts, 1949. Print.

Michelli, Joseph A. *The Starbucks Experience: 5 Principles for Turning Ordinary into Extraordinary.* New York: McGraw-Hill, 2007. Print.

Naish, John. *Enough: Breaking Free from the World of More*. London: Hodder & Stoughton, 2008. Print.

Pine, B. Joseph., and James H. Gilmore. *The Experience Economy Work Is Theatre & Every Business a Stage*. Boston: Harvard Business School, 1999. Print.

Pink, Daniel H. *A Whole New Mind: Why Right-brainers Will Rule the Future*. New York: Riverhead, 2006. Print.

Putnam, Robert D. *Bowling Alone: The Collapse and Revival of American Community*. New York: Simon & Schuster, 2000. Print.

Richo, David. *How to Be an Adult: A Handbook on Psychological and Spiritual Integration*. New York: Paulist, 1991. Print.

Ries, Eric. *The Lean Startup: How Today's Entrepreneurs Use Continuous Innovation to Create Radically Successful Businesses*. New York: Crown Business, 2011. Print.

Rifkin, Jeremy. *The Third Industrial Revolution: How Lateral Power Is Transforming Energy, the Economy, and the World*. New York: Palgrave Macmillan, 2011. Print.

Rifkin, Jeremy. *Zero Marginal Cost Society: The Rise of the Collaborative Commons and the End of Capitalism*. N.p.: n.p., n.d. Print.

Rubin, Jeff. *The End of Growth*. Toronto: Random House Canada, 2012. Print.

Snow, Richard. *I Invented the Modern Age: The Rise of Henry Ford*. New York: Simon & Schuster, n.d. Print.

Sommers, Sam. *Situations Matter: Understanding How Context Transforms Your World*. New York: Riverhead, 2011. Print.

Thaler, Richard H. *Misbehaving: The Making of Behavioural Economics*. London: Lane, 2015. Print.

Thomas, Martin. *Loose: The Future of Business Is Letting Go*.

London: Headline, 2011. Print.

Toffler, Alvin, and Heidi Toffler. *Revolutionary Wealth*. New York: Knopf, 2006. Print.

Toffler, Alvin. *The Third Wave*. New York: Morrow, 1980. Print.

Wilber, Ken. *A Theory of Everything: An Integral Vision for Business, Politics, Science, and Spirituality*. Boston: Shambhala, 2000. Print.

ABOUT BILL BISHOP

Bill Bishop is the CEO of **Bishop Communications Inc**. and the creator of **The BIG Idea Adventure™**, an advanced coaching program that helps entrepreneurs grow their business by creating, packaging, and promoting BIG Ideas. During the past 20 years, more than 10,000 entrepreneurs have graduated from his membership programs.

In addition to this book, Bill Bishop is the author of **How To Sell A Lobster** (now sold in 25 countries in 12 languages), **The Problem With Penguins**, **Beyond Basketballs**, and **Global Marketing For The Digital Age**. He was also the author of **Strategic Marketing For The Digital Age**, the first book ever published about e-commerce and Internet marketing.

Bill is also the founder of two social networks—**The 10% Referral Club™** and **The Keynote Collective™**, and the inventor of the board game **Quibberish®: The Paraphrase Puzzle Game**.

Bill has delivered speeches to hundreds of organizations including The MIT Entrepreneur Program, TEC, Entrepreneur's Organization (EO), Advocis, The Knowledge Bureau, MDRT, NAIFA, NAPFA, Independent Financial Brokers, Workcomp Advisors, Pro-Seminars, BNI, The Ivey School of Business, The Schulich School of Business, and Queen's University Executive MBA Program.

To reach Bill, call 647.436.8829 or email bill@bishopbigideas.com

You can also visit: BishopBIGIdeas.com

13268312R00131

Made in the USA
San Bernardino, CA
13 December 2018